THE MIRACULOUS LIFE OF
Maggie
the
WUNDERDOG

KASEY CARLIN

m B

MIRROR BOOKS

First published by Mirror Books in 2020
This paperback edition published in 2020

Mirror Books is part of Reach plc
10 Lower Thames Street
London EC3R 6EN

www.mirrorbooks.co.uk

ISBN 978-1-913406-34-9

Typeset by Danny Lyle

Printed and bound in Great Britain by
CPI Group (UK) Ltd, Croydon, CR0 4YY

A CIP catalogue record for this book is available from the British Library.

Plate section photos courtesy of Hussein, founder of Mashala Shelter (page 1).

1 3 5 7 9 10 8 6 4 2

THE MIRACULOUS LIFE OF

Maggie
the
WUNDERDOG

To my mum (Maggie's grandma), who always taught me to be kind, no matter someone's abilities or outward appearance.

"It doesn't matter what someone looks like,
all that matters is what's inside their heart."

PROLOGUE
2018

"Kasey, you have to see this."

My mum looked up from her phone and beckoned me over, a pained expression on her face.

"What is it?"

"A dog, a beautiful one. Poor love."

Dog photos! Mum certainly knows how to get my attention. Excited but confused at the sadness in her voice, I went over and sat down beside her.

"I've just seen this Facebook post from the Wild at Heart Foundation," she sighed. "Brace yourself, it's pretty hard reading."

She passed me the phone.

Angie is a street dog from Beirut who has suffered extensive abuse, the post began. *We are asking you to help us bring her to the UK, where she can start her life over with people who will love and care for her and where she can learn that most humans have good hearts.*

My heart bled for the poor creature already. I have always loved dogs, and can't stand the idea of them being mistreated. Ever since I started rescuing, my drive to help animals in need has just got stronger and stronger.

I read on.

Angie is blind; her eyes have been completely gouged out. She has also had one of her ears cut off. She has suffered severe trauma and needs patience and understanding to overcome her past. Sadly this is unlikely to happen if she remains in Beirut.

At the bottom of the post was a picture of a beautiful blonde mongrel. She was looking away from the camera, her head lowered. Her face told a story of exhaustion and hopelessness. I looked closer. Where her gleaming eyes should have been, there was nothing but two dark spaces. Her left ear pointed flatly sideways, but her right ear was nowhere to be seen. She was a gorgeous dog. But she looked like she had given up.

I was in love. "She's wonderful," I said to Mum. "I so hope someone can help her."

"They're looking for a home for her at the moment," Mum replied, "once they've raised enough money to bring her to the UK. What do you think?"

"Think about what?"

"Taking her in?"

"What? How on earth could I manage that?" I looked at Mum disbelievingly.

I was already dealing with one rescue dog, and she was proving a real handful. Mishka had serious behavioural issues and I was doing some pretty intensive training with her. She was draining enough on her own – but I had no intention of giving up on her.

"There's no way I could manage another dog, Mum."

I at least needed to iron out Mishka's issues before I thought about getting another dog – even just a foster dog who I might then pass on to another owner. Mishka was such an attention-vacuum at that time I didn't know how I would manage with two. Mishka is an Alaskan Klee Klai, a very fancy breed from America. She is like a miniature husky, and has a real husky temperament – quite aloof, but super-intelligent and absolutely exhausting.

Over the following days, though, Angie the one-eared dog kept popping up in my mind. I couldn't stop checking back into the Wild At Heart page for updates on her progress. I wanted to know what colour her eyes had been before she'd so cruelly lost them. I wanted to help that poor, hunched creature, who must have been in so much pain. And I wanted to know that she had a safe, loving home to come to in the UK.

I watched the videos of her as they were posted online. They broke my heart. In one of them, she was cowering in the corner of a sofa, huddled up as if to avoid the camera. She looked too scared to move. I might not have been able to see the fear in her eyes, but her body language said it all. She looked like she was trying to hide inside herself. In each video, she was constantly panting, which I knew to be a sign of stress in dogs. She flinched at the slightest noise.

I couldn't stand feeling so helpless, thinking about what she was going through.

In another video, one of the dog rescuers tried to look into her eyes to see how badly they had been affected. He gently tried to lift her head and she kept burying her face into his chest because she was so afraid he was going to cause her pain. She was clearly terrified of humans, and I felt anger boiling up inside me just thinking about the cruelty that people must have inflicted on her in the past.

It was so hard to watch. The sounds she was making were heart-shatteringly awful. Her whole body seemed to be saying, "Just love me. I don't care what you do, but please don't hurt me."

I couldn't get her out of my head. I kept thinking about how sore her eyes looked, and about her cute wonky jaw and her round tummy. Sadly, I knew she wasn't going to be at the top of anyone's doggie wish list.

The posts about Angie the dog always mentioned how scared and nervous she was. She needed a lot of special attention, and I think that must have been putting people off adopting her. Rehabilitating her, helping her to trust humans again, would be a huge job for anyone to take on.

As the days went by, I realised that my Mishka's training was actually coming along really well. She was learning so quickly, and I began to feel more confident that I perhaps I could manage another dog after all. I couldn't leave Angie out in the cold, knowing that nobody had stepped in to foster her. And I knew that the best way to train a dog is to allow it to face the very things it's afraid of. Sometimes we overcome our issues because of the things that happen to us, not in spite of them. And I wanted to make that happen for Angie.

She hadn't been a part of my life plan. But neither had Mishka – she had come along entirely by chance – and if I could make a success of adopting her, there was no reason I shouldn't be the one to give Angie a second chance in life.

And ultimately, I knew I'd want to carry on fostering dogs soon enough. I hadn't been intending to take one on right at that moment, but I had intended to as and when I could manage it. The more I thought about Angie, the more I had to make it happen. I hadn't known a thing about this blonde bombshell until six days before she came into my life, but I felt sure that she would change it forever.

I discussed it with Mum, and she knew Angie had won me over and I had to do something. She talked me round. So I contacted Wild At Heart, offering to be Angie's sponsor mum.

They were delighted, and we drew up a plan. Angie would come and live with me as a long-term foster dog, and once she was rehabilitated I'd eventually pass her on to a permanent owner. As she wasn't conventionally beautiful, I suspected that might take a while. But all the time, I was secretly hoping that my mum would fall in love with her and want to adopt her. I had a gut feeling that if she stayed with us long enough, Mum wouldn't want to let her go, so my cunning ruse was to make Angie a part of our family until we had no choice but to take her in full-time.

I wanted to teach Angie to trust again, and I wanted her to know what it meant to be loved. It would be a case of taking things slowly but surely, but I felt sure she would find it in herself to realise that there were kind people out there who would show her affection and feed her, not just abuse or hurt her.

I wasn't sure about the name Angie, though. I thought she deserved something a bit cuter.

CHAPTER ONE

A LUCKY ESCAPE

It's a scorching day in Beirut and a scruffy blonde dog is lying with her head hanging low, chained to a wire crate. Her stomach is bloated due to the puppies she's expecting, and she can't move to forage for food. She relies on the man she can hear walking about to ensure she doesn't starve.

To make matters worse, she has no idea where she is. Her eyes, once a beautiful autumnal shade of orangey-brown, are now completely closed, glued together by the infection that has ravaged them.

At some point her jaw has been broken, and her left ear has been savagely removed, leaving a misshapen patch of fur-covered cartilage.

If you stroked her you would feel some of the tiny bullets that are still lodged inside of her, and if you were to cuddle her you would sense just how badly she is craving love and security.

This is the story of not only one of the most loving, but also one of the luckiest dogs in the world. Her journey starts on the streets of Lebanon, where she was just one of many, many street dogs with no name, no family and no home. I don't know where or when she was born, but I do know she spent around two years on the streets before being rescued.

And when she was, this poor, gorgeous dog was clinging to life by the skin of her teeth.

Her first stroke of luck came through a man called Hussein, who runs a dog shelter in the countryside outside Beirut. Hussein has helped rehabilitate countless dogs on their way to happier lives. And in Lebanon, that's not an easy task. There are a lot of animal lovers in Lebanon, but a lot of people see dogs – especially street dogs – as a nuisance. There is a real problem with animal over-population there, as people very rarely neuter their dogs, so the problem grows and grows.

Because of this, street dogs are often treated like we would treat rats and pigeons – as if they are vermin. Many people simply think there are too many of them and they get in the way. If you saw a pigeon walking around with one leg in the UK, it's unlikely you would pick it up and take it home to look after it. But with the population problem in Lebanon, that's how many people naturally react to suffering dogs. To them, it's normal to see a dog in a bad state, because that's what they've grown up around.

And that's what makes the work that Hussein does all the more astonishing. Sadly, it's rare for animals to be rehabilitated in Lebanon, and population control is rarely humane. A lot of dogs are simply dumped out in the countryside if they're no longer wanted. Stray or aggressive animals are sometimes shot by animal control officers, or even fed food laced with poison. It's unthinkable to us, but until recently there were no animal cruelty laws in Lebanon, so there were no consequences for mistreating animals. Thankfully, there are also amazing people like Hussein doing some amazing work.

One day, Hussein got a call from a friend, saying he'd found a dog who had been severely mistreated and was in desperate need of help. She was horrifically injured, starving and pregnant. Hussein didn't think twice. He went out to pick her up immediately, and took her back to his shelter.

Hussein couldn't be sure what had happened to her, because she was in such a terrible state. But feeling her rough fur riddled with tiny lumps and bumps beneath his fingers, he could only imagine what she might have been through.

It was clear that the dog had been shot. Not just once, not twice, but a countless number of times. The most likely scenario made Hussein feel sick to his stomach. He had heard horror stories before about dogs in Lebanon who had been tied up and used for target practice. As unimaginable as that sounded, the number of bullets he could feel inside this dog suggested it could be the case.

Another possibility was that kids shot her because she was a stray. Or perhaps she had been exploited for breeding, and her eyes had been shot out so she couldn't run away. That would explain her pregnancy, which was plain to see. But she looked like a mongrel, not a pedigree dog, so her puppies couldn't have been very profitable. The most likely situation, then, was that this poor creature had been attacked at random and shot at by strangers.

Examining her face, Hussein concluded she must have been attacked at least twice: her ear appeared to have been brutally cut off, rather than shot off, so that must have happened in a separate incident. She also had scarring on her head, which could have been down to more violence inflicted by humans or fights with other dogs. Hussein knew how limited food could be for stray dogs like her, and how viciously strays would fight each other for scraps, just to stay alive.

Her jaw had been broken at some point and had reset in a wonky position – another sign that she had been beaten or kicked, or perhaps even hit by a car. Hussein's heart broke just looking at her, and he approached her carefully, caught hold of the terrified creature and cradled her as he picked her up.

She was terrified and skittish on the journey back, and was agitated by being around people, because of the intense trauma she had suffered. So when they arrived at the shelter, Hussein put a chain on her to stop her running away. He was determined to keep hold of her until she got the help she needed and found a new home.

But already Hussein was faced with a terrible decision. He knew that when the dog gave birth, no one would want to take on the puppies. They would have terrible lives ahead of them, and would almost definitely end up on the streets. It would only add to the existing problems with overpopulation and animal cruelty, and it didn't seem fair to inflict on them the terrible pain and suffering that their mother had already endured.

So he made the kindest decision he could, at that time and in that place, as heartbreaking as it was. Sadly, her pregnancy had to be terminated. Those poor little pups would have had no hope.

When her pregnancy was terminated she was also neutered, for her own safety and wellbeing. On examination, Hussein determined that she had already had one litter previously, and goodness knows what happened to those poor dogs. It just wasn't fair to leave more little puppies to fend for themselves if she had another liaison with another dog – which happened often between dogs kept together in rescue centres. Hussein just didn't have the funds to keep and feed them all.

The poor creature's eyes were still open when she arrived at the rescue centre, but they were essentially just cavities. So Hussein took her to the vet, where she was given antibiotics to clear up the infection that had ravaged her eye sockets. He knew that her eyes would have to be closed permanently at a later date.

But Hussein also knew that the cost of ongoing surgery was going to pose a serious problem for him. As dedicated as he was to his animals and his work, Hussein simply didn't have the funds to carry on paying for vet bills. So as a next step, he decided to post on several Facebook rescue groups, to see if there was anyone out there who would be better placed to help this creature in such desperate need. He knew in his heart a traumatised, suffering dog like her deserved a second chance – as he believed all rescue dogs did. All she needed was someone to believe in her.

Her second stroke of luck came through a woman called Roxanna, 2,000 miles away in the UK. Roxanna was sitting in the bath when she saw Hussein's post and the accompanying picture, and she cried for an hour because this beautiful, blonde, blind dog looked so sad. She didn't know how she was going to help, but she knew she had to.

Roxanna had rescued her own dog, Cookie, from Lebanon, and she wanted to try and do what she could to help this one as well. At a time when Hussein couldn't afford to keep her any longer, no one else cared, and the poor dog was entirely alone in the world, Roxanna stepped in and saved her life. She saw past her defects, her shyness, her wonky jaw – and she opened her heart to her.

Roxanna began reaching out to animal charities to ask for help. It was hard going, as many viewed this scarred, traumatised dog as a lost cause. She couldn't find anyone to take her, and some people she contacted even said it would be kinder to put the creature down. All they saw was a blind dog who had had its ear hacked off, and they knew how hard it could be to even just to get healthy dogs rehomed in the UK.

It was only when she contacted an amazing dog charity called Wild At Heart that Roxanna finally struck gold, another link in the chain of miracles keeping this scruffy mongrel alive. A lady called Eve replied to Roxanna to say they would help. At that moment, an enormous weight lifted from Roxanna's shoulders. She had never felt relief like it.

An amazing lady called Nikki Tibbles runs the Wild at Heart Foundation. She's a full-time dog lover who has travelled all over the world, rescuing dogs and introducing neutering programmes to help stem the increase in strays (at the last count there were a whopping 600 million stray dogs worldwide).

The work Nikki and her team do has prevented hundreds of thousands more puppies being born into a life of misery, hunger and mistreatment. Spay-a-thons may sound callous, but neutering really is the only humane way to keep the dog population healthy. Incredibly, one litter of un-neutered dogs can result in 67,000 dogs in six years, and you can bet those poor little mites won't have a good run of it.

Nikki is on a mission to lower the number of dogs suffering from neglect in any way she can, and a neglected dog, abandoned and broken on the streets of Lebanon, was the perfect case for the Wild at Heart Foundation to step in on.

The first step for Roxanna and Wild At Heart was to get the dog into a foster home. Roxanna's dog Cookie had stayed in a home before she adopted her, so she contacted the owner to enquire about doing the same again. Farah, the woman who fostered Cookie, had very little money and already had six dogs of her own – but she loved animals so much that over time she very kindly became a stepping-stone between rescue centres in Lebanon and the UK.

The plan was for this new dog to stay with Farah until Roxanna could raise some funds and get the paperwork in order to bring her over to the UK. There was another dog Roxanna wanted to rescue at the same time, and the cost for bringing both of them over was going to be around £5,000.

First things first, this poor dog needed a name if they were to rehome her. Eventually, they settled on Angie – a fitting name for this angelic but hopelessly timid creature. The priority for Farah, Roxanna and Wild At Heart was to make Angie as comfortable as possible in the company of humans as her rehabilitation began. So Angie didn't leave

Farah's house for six whole months in her care, in order to help her readjust to a world in which she wouldn't be beaten and tortured.

There was a lot of work to do to help rehabilitate poor Angie, but a big part of her initial recovery involved a simple cardboard box, which she was given to use as a bed. That box became her sanctuary. She finally felt like she had a safe place, where nobody would hurt her and she could rest without being disturbed. Once Angie had somewhere to call home, Farah found that this scared, damaged street dog gradually began to accept Farah's help and to trust her just a little more.

The politics and costs involved in bringing dogs to the UK can be enormously time consuming, but while Farah was doing her best to improve Angie's condition, Roxanna and Wild At Heart managed to raise enough for Angie to go to a local vet in Lebanon and have her eyes permanently closed. Again, this would help her live a more comfortable life, without the constant risk of infection.

It was when the vet went in to clean out Angie's eye sockets that he found two bullets in each side. They were removed, her eye sockets were fully cleaned out, and then her eyelids were fused together. Her right eye was very badly damaged so there wasn't much skin to work with, so it had to be shut much tighter than her left one.

Roxanna persisted in her campaign to raise more money to fly Angie back to Britain, and to find her somewhere to live. It wasn't viable for her to keep Angie herself at that time, because she had already taken on the responsibility of looking after Cookie in her flat. But if she couldn't foster her on her own, she was determined to find someone who could.

And it was not long afterwards that Mum showed me the Wild At Heart post on Facebook, I saw a picture of Angie for the first time, and my life changed forever.

CHAPTER TWO
GENERAL ZAROFF

I've always been a dog person. But I didn't have a dog of my own for two years before I got Mishka in June 2018, and my scruffy Lebanese rescue was soon to follow.

What was I doing with my life before I got my girls? It was so boring! It wasn't as if there were no dogs in my life, though. I had started a doggie day-care business during those few years, walking and looking after dogs whose owners were working or away, and I love being around those crazy, wonderful creatures more than anything.

Animals were always part of my life in one way or another. Just like Angie, I moved around a lot when I was young. I was born in Scotland but grew up in America (my mum is Scottish and my dad is American). I've got an older brother and a younger sister, and I grew up mostly in Indiana, surrounded by cornfields and soybeans.

That was where my love of animals first began, and from a young age, if I saw a stray animal on the street I would pick it up and bring it home. I used to drive my dad crazy because I was constantly trying to help animals in situations where he didn't think I should get involved. When I got into my early teens I remember him saying to me, "Kasey, this has to stop. Even if you see Bambi lying in the road, leave him there!" But it simply wasn't in my nature.

As is the case in many cultures, attitudes to dogs in the US are different from ours in the UK. There are plenty of dogs who live their entire lives in backyards, or chained to dog houses – and it used to break my heart.

I knew I wanted to work with animals from way back when I was at pre-school. We had one those fun days where you dress up as what you want to be when you're older, and I went in wearing dungarees and a straw hat. I even took a little toy rabbit from my brother's magic set, and proudly declared, "I'm going to be the farmer and I'm going to raise animals!"

I knew from a young age that animals just get you. You don't have to say anything to them. You can just be with them, and that's enough. And for someone as shy as I was, that was exactly what I needed.

I think because we moved around so much when I was little, I found it really comforting being with animals. They felt very stable and loving. Not that I didn't have a stable and loving upbringing – because I really was blessed in so many ways. But my parents split up when I was very young, and my time was divided between them, as it is for a lot of kids. I don't remember it very well, but I guess I just felt a little uprooted at times, because I was back and forth a lot. Animals gave me the peace and stability I craved.

When I reached middle school, my mum moved to the UK with my younger sister, because she wanted to be nearer her family. I stayed in school in the US and lived with my dad and my older brother. Although I missed my mum and sister, animals – and especially dogs – were my constant companions.

The first dog we had was a German Shepherd called Zaroff (or General Zaroff to give him his full title) that my dad rescued from a shelter when I was about eight. He was named after a man from a book called *The Greatest Hunter*, and he was such a great dog.

Dad chose Zaroff because when he initially went to the shelter to get a dog, he walked past all the cages and asked the dogs to sit. Because they were so excited to see a human being, they were all jumping up at the doors – but Zaroff just sat there quietly and my dad instantly thought, "that's the dog for me."

He didn't have the money on him to pay for Zaroff, but he assured the people at the rescue centre that he would be back the following day.

But when he went back with the cash the next day, he found that they hadn't taken him at his word. Zaroff had gone.

Shockingly, the shelter had what's known as a "three-day kill rule". It was a disturbingly common policy in the US, whereby if the dogs weren't claimed after three days, they would be euthanised.

My dad was devastated. But after falling in love with Zaroff, he now had his heart set on getting a German Shepherd. So off he went to a specialist German Shepherd rescue centre in the next town.

And guess who was there waiting for him?

Zaroff's life had been saved, and he came to live with us from that day onwards.

Zaroff was an extraordinarily calm and stoic dog. Nothing could ruffle him. We suspected that he was trained for personal protection or police work, because he was so well disciplined. Dogs would run up to him growling and barking and he wouldn't even flinch. He'd just like stand there and take it. The only thing he didn't like was men in uniforms – another reason we thought maybe he was a protection dog. Perhaps he was a bit scared because he wasn't treated very well. The difficulty with rescue dogs is that you never know exactly what's gone on in their past, and they can be unpredictable and difficult to manage as a result.

But Zaroff was trained to perfection. He would always stay to heel, and was always responsive. Nowadays I always say you can't get a dog without expecting to train it, but Zaroff was unbelievable and we didn't have to do a thing.

My dad worked as a teacher at the local university. He drove a Jeep with an open top, and one day a student saw Dad walk off without locking his car. He asked him if he was going to secure it and my dad replied, "No it's fine, I've got my own security system."

Then General Zaroff poked his head out of the window, and the guy's eyes widened. "Oh, I see," he stammered.

On one occasion my dad and brother were playing American football in the garden, and my dad threw the football at my brother and jokingly said, "Zaroff, go and get him!" Zaroff went straight over and grabbed my brother's t-shirt, and held him there. He didn't growl and he wasn't aggressive – he just made sure my brother stayed put. He looked at my dad with my brother's top hanging out of his mouth as if to say, "What do you want me to do now?"

I could walk down the street and Zaroff wouldn't leave my side. He used to sleep on my bed, and at some point in the night he would get up and go and sit in the middle of the staircase so he could guard both the top and bottom of the house.

I remember thinking when I was about 10, "I wonder when he gets off the bed? Does he just wait until I fall asleep?"

So I closed my eyes and I pretended to be was asleep – and as soon as I did that Zaroff got off my bed and went and sat on the stairs. That was the moment I realised how fiercely loyal dogs are, and I swelled up with love and pride at how far Zaroff would go to keep us safe.

Sadly he died from cancer when he was about eight and I was around 12. He was a beautiful beast – but it's funny, because when I look at pictures of him now he's not how I remember at all. In my head he was a strong, young, handsome hunk of a dog, but now I realise he was actually a bit of a chubster with lots of grey hairs around his muzzle.

I was so sad when Zaroff died. You can't beat growing up with a dog like that. He was the first pup I loved, and it's no wonder I've loved them ever since.

CHAPTER THREE
ANGIE ARRIVES

It was September 2018 when Roxanna finally raised enough money to bring Angie over to the UK. She had to fly out to Lebanon to collect her, and they drove two hours to the airport in a hire car with Angie sat in the footwell (they're not big on safety over there). At the airport, Angie's papers and passport were checked, and then she was put into a travel crate and loaded onto the plane.

I did so much research in the weeks leading up to my new foster doggie coming over, and made sure I was as prepared as I could be. I learnt that the best thing to do with blind dogs initially is to keep them in one room, so they don't get too confused in a new place. It's also a good idea to put a baby gate across the door so they can hear everything that is going on in the other rooms, but can't go into them.

Once the dog is more comfortable with being in one room and they know their way around, you can move them to another room and put the baby gate over that door. My plan was to take everything very slowly and steadily. Because I had fostered plenty of dogs before, I knew how everything else would work, and I had things in place and ready for Angie, with a big crate and lots of food and blankets for maximum comfort. She was going to need it after her 2,000-mile journey.

Getting on a plane must have been a strange sensation for a street dog who couldn't see or understand what was happening to her. Would her one ear pop like ours do when the plane took off? She couldn't have any idea she was miles above the earth. Would she realise she was in a different country when she landed in London? Would it smell different? Would the ground feel different beneath her feet?

The checks she had to go through before getting on the plane were absolutely crucial. Roxanna has since tried to bring another rescue called Trinity over to Britain, but when she got to the airport Trinity wasn't allowed to fly because his rabies vaccination was two days late. But checks like these are vital to ensure we don't have a rabies problem in the UK. Any dog coming from a country at risk need rigorous checks, and it's a long process to prove that the dogs are risk-free. That's part of the reason why it had taken months for poor Angie to get clearance to fly over. (Thankfully, Trinity has also finally been cleared and is living happily in Canada now.)

The flight is just over five hours, and must have been confusing as hell. This suffering, broken creature was travelling towards a brighter future, but she wouldn't have known where she was, and the sensation when the plane took off and landed must have been distressing and uncomfortable.

Angie and Roxanna landed at 5pm, and I had driven to Heathrow to meet them off the plane. Roxanna came out to meet me in the reception area, and then the really long wait for Angie began. We knew the most complicated part of the process would start when she was unloaded from the plane and sent through UK border checks.

The UK have an extremely strict import and export system, and as difficult as it might sound, all dogs have to be left in kennels for several hours to make sure they're healthy and not stressed. The animal centre is totally separate from the airport for safety's sake, which only adds to the waiting time. Roxanna and I were on edge for hour after hour, praying that everything would be okay. There was always a chance that she would be refused entry.

I was nervous about meeting Angie for the first time. She had only met Roxanna the day before, and I didn't know how comfortable she'd yet be around humans. I imagined that the last thing Angie had seen before she went blind was a person – probably a vicious, abusive one at that, given what happened to her. So a part of me was concerned that she would be standoffish or aggressive with people. Especially given the disorientating new circumstances and the change of scene, I was really anxious to make her as comfortable as possible. I just wanted to be able to give her a hug, tell her everything would be okay, and bring her into the safety of my home.

I thought the best thing for Angie was for me to let her and Roxanna have a bit of time together before Roxanna introduced me. I expected that she would be shaking and cowering like I had seen her in the videos, and that she'd need the comfort of somebody familiar, even if she hadn't known Roxanna that long, before meeting yet another stranger. So I decided to take a step back until I could see that she trusted Roxanna with whatever was going to happen next.

The checking process was so extensive that Angie didn't appear until after 10pm, five hours after the plane had touched down. And when she did, I was stunned.

This wasn't the shy, battered dog I had expected. The door to the animal centre suddenly opened, and this beautiful one-eared bundle of joy came high-kicking towards us, feeling her way forward on the ground in front of her. She didn't seem so badly affected by her arduous journey after all. She was curiously sniffing the air and had a look about her as if she was searching around for someone to cuddle. She was just adorable. My heart melted.

Roxanna was so happy to see Angie again that she started bawling her eyes out. The staff at the animal centre in Heathrow must have seen so many animals come and go over the years, but even they were breaking down in tears at the sight of this blind, one-eared, wonky dog snuggling up to Roxanna to give her a cuddle.

I gave them a few minutes, but I couldn't resist much longer. I tentatively walked over and knelt down close to her. She was much smaller than I expected. Her face had been shaved because of her recent eye operation, and she still had scabs on her eyelids. She came over and nuzzled her bald little face into my shoulder, and I could feel her gently shaking. She'd been through the worst of her operations and she was beginning a new phase of healing and a new life of love and care, but it still must have been so painful.

She was the total opposite of what I'd expected. Bearing in mind her past, she was an astonishingly loving and trusting creature. All she wanted was affection. And the second I took her into my arms and cuddled her for the first time, I was in bits. I couldn't stop crying about how beautiful she was. She had this incredible warmth that seemed to radiate and swallow up everyone around her. To me, she was perfection. As soon as I met her it was like she was saying to me, "Here I am. You're going to love me." I didn't need any convincing.

It doesn't take much to make me cry, but this was one of the most beautiful moments I had ever felt with an animal. I couldn't believe how well this poor, beaten, abused dog was taking everything in her stride. She had suffered so much for so long, but now she seemed just to accept her reality and go with whatever was happening.

She was quite a funny shape, bless her. She had really big saggy nipples due to her pregnancies, and had a big roll of fat covering her bum. When she wagged her tail the fat jiggled about – and I didn't want to break it to her so early on, but I knew she needed to go on a diet.

She weighed 26 kg, which was a lot for a dog of her size. That may sound surprising for a dog who had been treated so badly, and in truth she was the first overweight street dog I'd ever seen. But I reminded myself that she had spent the past six months sat inside, hardly moving – so her size wasn't really so astonishing after all. I knew how much better a shape she was in than when she was first rescued. Her weight had all gathered around her chest and belly, and because she hadn't been using her legs that much, they didn't have much muscle mass, so she was like a barrel on sticks.

The staff around us were deeply moved by the scene of love and affection playing out before their eyes, and they started asking me about her back story. But I was still crying too much to talk, so Roxanna had to fill them in.

I guess when you've been through as much as Angie has, nothing fazes you anymore. She had a good sniff around when she arrived in the reception area, and I knew at that moment that we'd be able to make her feel at home with me. She seemed capable of making the best of every situation. She didn't seem at all fearful or nervous as I had anticipated, and despite having been on the go for 16 hours, she was unbelievably relaxed and accepting of what was happening to her.

Of course, just like humans, dogs are deeply affected by things that have happened to them in the past, and I had to pinch myself as a reminder of what she had been through. I knew our journey together wouldn't all be plain sailing. But as for Angie, she didn't seem to be thinking past her next meal. I suppose that's just how dogs are. They don't ponder the meaning of life, dwell on the past, or worry about where they're going to be in five years' time. They probably assume they'll have the same owner, still be curled up in the same bed, and be served their dinner at 6pm for the rest of their lives. And I was determined to give this lovely pup all of those things, so that she could finally become a normal dog again.

CHAPTER FOUR
TED AND ROXY

I had some previous experience with animals who were partially sighted. Not long ago we had a family dog called Ted, a Yorkie, who went blind in his old age. He had cataracts and lost his sight over time so, it was a different scenario from the one Angie found herself in. But we had still had to adapt things for Ted, so I knew a bit about caring for a sight-challenged dog.

Ted still had some vision in his final years but it was cloudy, and the main things we had to do was make sure we didn't move the furniture around so we didn't confuse him, and we took care not to approach him too quickly so as not to frighten him. He had to relearn a lot of the things he had previously taken for granted, like knowing when other dogs were around or where objects were, but he managed it. He still lived a very happy life for a couple of years after his sight went, so we knew it was possible for blind dogs to be fulfilled.

The older he got, the more hilariously grumpy Ted became, and if he didn't like something, he would let you know by whipping his head round and trying to nip you like a cat.

Ted and Roxy, Mum's other dog, were like husband and wife. We adopted them as a pair after their owner fell ill and they had to be rehomed. Ted and Roxy absolutely loved each other. They spent all of their time together, but as Ted got older and less capable, there came a time when Roxy started telling Ted off – something that she had never done before.

We could tell it really distressed Ted, because he didn't understand why it was happening. Neither did we – but Ted had always ruled the roost, so we suspected that she was taking advantage of the fact he had become weaker, so started to assert her dominance.

Ted seemed to be losing his spark, and it wasn't fair on him or Roxy being in a situation where they weren't getting on anymore. And when you start to realise that your dog is unhappy, that's the time you really have to think about what's best for them, and not what's best for you. We had adapted to his difficulties with seeing and responding to people and other animals, but seeing his quality of life decline at home forced us to make the most difficult choice of all.

Ted was almost 19 when we made the heart-breaking decision to have him put down. He was just too unwell to go on, and it was the kindest thing we could have done. It had nothing to do with his sight – but Mum and I both knew that it was Ted's time to cross over the rainbow bridge.

Even though he was a very old man and was unwell, he didn't lose his fighting spirit and kept up his bad boy reputation right to the end. When the vet gave him the initial injection to make him drowsy, he turned around sharply and tried to bite her. He had no teeth left by that point, but he still gave it a go. Then when she tried to attach the canula, he went to bite her again. He was such a funny boy. He was a feisty little thing – a typical terrier. Ted taught me so much about how to look after a dog when they are most in need, and that lesson was going to be as valuable as any when Angie came into my life.

My mum still has Roxy, who we think is a Jack Russell-Chihuahua cross. As with many rescues, it's hard to know for sure. She's black and tan with really big ears, and she's really long, so I do wonder if there's a bit of sausage dog in her too. My mum is also fostering a little mixed-breed girl called Cleo at the moment, who I think has Shi-Tzu in her.

And then there's Fudge.

Fudge is my mum's cat, but I swear she acts more like a dog. When Mum and I used to get the bus into Brighton, she would walk us down to the bus stop. Then when we got the bus home, she would be waiting at the bus stop on the other side of the street for us. She's loyal as anything.

When my mum used to walk to work, she would walk the whole 45-minute journey with her, and then wait for her and walk her home – like a polite gentleman from the 1950s.

My mum even got a call from my sister's school once asking her to go and collect Fudge because she'd followed my sister all the way to school, and then tried to join her for lessons.

She's old now, bless her, and all she wants to do these days is lie in the back garden in the sunshine. But in her youth, she was a real adventurer. She brought us back a pheasant she'd caught once. It was twice the size of her because she's only a diddy little thing, but she was fearless in her youth.

So there were plenty of animals for Angie to meet when she got home, but I knew from experience that we would have to take things slowly. Despite her initial assuredness,

I would have to work extra hard to make her as relaxed as possible. There could be all sorts of hidden trauma that might only emerge later, and it certainly wouldn't all be smooth going. I had a crate for her in the back of my van, ready for the two-hour drive back, and I was determined to make it as easy for her as possible on the journey and once we arrived.

But as I took her out of the animal centre at Heathrow, I realised there was another pressing issue that I needed to think about.

CHAPTER FIVE
MAGGIE COMES TO STAY

As soon as I set eyes on her, I knew instinctively that Angie wasn't the right name for my lovely Lebanese rescue. It was cute, but a little too formal for my liking. I didn't have any immediate great ideas for a more suitable name, but as she was going through a reinvention of her own, I thought it right she should have a new name to go with her new life.

So on the way home in the van I started chatting to her about what she wanted to be called.

She was lying on the passenger seat next to me. I had brought the crate to put her in in the back, but when I thought about what she'd just been through, what with the long flight and being stuck in the kennels, I wanted to give her a cosier experience on the last leg of her trip. So I put her on the passenger seat next to me, attaching her to the seatbelt using her harness. She immediately settled down and curled her paws underneath her, and that was the first time I saw her properly exhale. She looked tired but content, her closed eyes twitching inquisitively.

I chatted to her the whole way home so she didn't feel scared. I thought if I distracted her, the unfamiliar surroundings and my unfamiliar presence wouldn't be as traumatic.

And eventually I came round to the big question.

"So what are we going to call you, gorgeous? Sunshine?"

My mum had suggested Sunshine, and it seemed perfect for such a radiant dog, who had lit up the whole room at the airport.

"Sunshine?"

She exhaled again and shuffled a little in her seat. Sunshine wasn't a goer, then.

"How about Margot? Margot?" I trilled, sing-songing her name to get her attention.

I liked the idea of Margot, after Margot Robbie. This dog had been through a rough time, but I was damned if she wasn't one of the most beautiful creatures I'd ever seen.

Her ear twitched, but it was only a flicker of interest. She seemed firmly unimpressed by Margot. Perhaps I needed something a bit chirpier.

I racked my brains. My sister had mentioned the name Maggie, because she really likes the character Maggie in *The Walking Dead*. It seemed a bit of a morbid choice to me, though it was definitely a cute name. And it was near enough to Margot, but slightly more fun.

I ran through the name ideas once again, just to make sure.

"Angie?"

She raised her head, slightly mournfully, and shyly turned her muzzle in my direction.

"Sunshine?"

She looked around, lost interest and lowered her head back down onto her paws.

"Margot?"

No response. She definitely wasn't a Margot.

"Maggie!"

She snapped to attention and let out a little squeak. I glanced at her, taking my eyes off the road for the slightest moment, and it was like she was really looking at me. Her little closed eyelids were twitching with interest again, and she cocked her head to one side.

"Maggie!"

She whined a little louder this time, and nosed about for my arm on the gearstick.

"Well, I think that's decided then, isn't it, Maggie!"

I couldn't keep the smile off my face. My lovely chubby Lebanese mutt had survived the worst, and this felt like a real step forward in bringing her back to normality again. She probably liked the sound of Maggie just because it was similar enough to Angie, but all that mattered was that she responded to it and didn't seem anxious about it.

And so it stuck. Maggie was coming to stay.

Maggie was good on the lead from the word go. She was much more a follower than a leader – which was, of course, totally understandable given that she couldn't see and had suddenly found herself in totally unfamiliar surroundings, with people and things that probably smelled weird to her and were strange to the touch. But she was very trusting in me, and she understood when she felt the pressure of a lead that it meant she needed to walk.

We didn't get back home until 12.30am. I didn't want to rush anything or unnerve Maggie, so I thought it was best just to put her out for a wee, before settling her down to sleep for the night.

So when we got back, the first thing I did was to plonk her on the grass outside so that she could do her business. Maggie proceeded to do the longest wee I had ever seen in my life. I wondered in disbelief if she had even had the chance to have one since leaving Lebanon. Perhaps she hadn't been able to go because of the nerves. In any case, she must have been bursting!

I imagine that Maggie must also have been very confused by the grass. Beirut is mainly made up of dusty roads, so it's unlikely she would have spent any time running around in freshly rained-on gardens. She stood there for ages smelling the grass, presumably trying to work out what it was and where on earth she was.

I carried Maggie's crate into the house and led her into it to go to bed. Mishka always slept on my bed, but as I'd only taken Maggie in until we found a permanent home for her, I had to make sure she was crate trained. Generally for an adoption to be a success, dogs have to be crate and toilet trained, or people won't want to take them on. It could create problems for her future owner if she expected to sleep in the same room as them and the owner didn't want that. So settling her into her crate was a priority.

I didn't introduce Maggie and Mishka to each other on the first night, as I didn't want Maggie's new surroundings to be too overwhelming. It was also very late, and bouncy Mishka might not do any of our energy levels much good right before bed. So I shut her in with plenty of blankets, and went to my room.

When I went to bed that night, all I could hear was Maggie softly whimpering. It was the saddest noise I'd ever heard. I got up a couple of times to comfort her and tell her that everything was okay, but I knew I would be setting myself up for failure if I spent all night cuddling her. She needed to learn to stand on her own four paws.

That was when it truly struck home that my beautiful Maggie was still a seriously traumatised dog. The second time I went to check on her, I found that she was whimpering in her sleep, and her little legs were running in the air. Through the darkness, I could tell she was asleep even though her eyes were closed all the time, because the muscles in her left eye wasn't twitching in the way it had at the sounds and smells around her during the day. But she seemed distressed even when dreaming, and I was convinced she was having nightmares about all the terrible things that had happened to her.

In the morning, I approached her very carefully and coaxed her out of her crate. Having previously taken in foster dogs, I knew that it was important to check over her physical state, to make sure I knew about anything that could be causing her discomfort. Quite apart from the obvious – her blindness and her missing ear – I noticed that her teeth weren't in the best condition. No one had ever looked after them or cared for them, so it was only natural that they wouldn't be in a good way. I knew how horrible it was to have toothache, and I could only imagine how awful it must be for dog to be going through that and not be able to express how much pain they're in.

Maggie had two broken teeth, but thankfully they hadn't become infected and the gums weren't exposed, so they weren't causing her a problem for the time being. I knew there was potential for them to become a problem further down the line, though, so I booked an appointment to get them removed. We would have to wait months, but it was a good idea to get in the queue now rather than letting her teeth become a problem before I did anything about it.

I gave Maggie a cuddle to reassure her that she was safe in her new home, and as I was massaging the skin around her neck, I felt a little bump beneath her fur that felt out of place. I made a note to ask the vet about it at our first appointment.

The next question I had to address was when to introduce her to Mishka, or to Mum's pets, since I was still living at home.

My usual way of introducing any dogs to each other is by taking them on a walk together so it's neutral ground, but I thought the morning after Maggie arrived in the UK was too soon to take her out into the big wide world, so I thought it would be a good idea to wear Mishka out a bit before I introduced them to each other. I decided to leave Maggie at home so she could settle in and get used to her new surroundings. My sister would stay at home with her and look after her. I would take Mishka on a really long walk with the other dogs I was looking after from my doggie day-care business. I would then go back to collect Maggie, and we'd have their first meeting away from home.

Mishka must have realised there was another dog in her home, but I still thought it was best to make sure she was a bit calmer than usual before I began formal introductions. Mishka is wired at times – if she were a human she would probably have an ASBO.

It was a quiet morning at work, so along with Mishka I only had Lennard, Lolli and Hector to take out for a spin. Lennard is a giant St Bernard, one of the biggest but most gentle dogs you could ever come across, and Hector is a very lively miniature Dachshund who befriends everyone, and Lennard's sister Lolli is half German Shepherd, half mystery. We had the full range of shapes and sizes that day.

I was curious as to how Maggie would settle in with my sister that morning. I was worried about her after her nighttime restlessness, and I really hoped that she'd be taking to her new surroundings. I'd asked my sister to take things incredibly slowly with her and be watchful after a traumatic few days and nights.

When I went back home to collect Maggie, I found her rolling around on the living room floor, playing with my sister. I was gobsmacked. No longer the terrified, huddled-up dog of the night before, she was even extending her neck so that my sister could scratch her favourite spots. All the stuff I'd been told by Maggie's rescuers about giving her time and space had gone right out of the window. Maggie had clearly decided that wasn't what she wanted.

Even better, she had already met Mum's cat, Fudge. That was the perfect preparation for meeting mad Mishka, because Fudge is gentler but also quite dominant. It could only be a good thing that Maggie had been exposed to our other pets in preparation for her big meet with Mishka. Maggie was used to being around cats because they have millions in Lebanon, but my sister said it hadn't all been plain sailing.

"Maggie went down really low," my sister said, "and tiptoed over to Fudge. As soon as Fudge meowed at her she backed right off." I reckoned Maggie had felt the wrath of cats before – she'd probably been swatted a few times in the past on the streets of Beirut.

She's also said hello to Mum's dog Roxy, who is basically like a potato. As Roxy is old now, she's so used to dogs coming in and out of the house that she was very nonplussed by Maggie.

I was delighted Maggie had made such good progress already. I picked her up and helped her into the back of the van. Mishka was riding shotgun. The rest of my day-care dogs piled into the car too, and we set off for the field where I planned to introduce Maggie and Mishka. Because Maggie could pick up all the other dogs' scents, she growled all the way there. Thankfully the other dogs were quite chilled out because we'd already been out walking for so long, so they weren't that fussed about Maggie. She was just another day-care dog to them.

Once I got her out of the car at the other end, she high-kicked her way into the field. To this day she still high-kicks when she's unsure and is trying to feel what's in front of her. It makes her look like a little show pony, and it's absolutely adorable.

I was going to keep Maggie on her own for a little while so she could acclimatise, but as soon as she got into the field she started investigating and going up to the other dogs and giving them a good sniff.

I had done my best to ease her into everything slowly, and I had been a little worried that interacting with a new group of dogs would be hard for her, but she followed me and the other dogs around like it was the most natural thing in the world. It was so instinctive.

I let her off the lead and she was soon snuffling around and getting used to the feeling of long grass underneath her feet. She was quite shy at first, of course, but she was also stubborn and determined. It was the perfect environment for her to flourish.

Maggie got on really well with all the other day-care dogs, but it was definitely not love at first sight for Maggie and Mishka. They tolerated each other, but that night when both girls were in the house together I could tell Mishka's nose had been put out of joint by the new arrival.

In those first few days, Maggie was very tentative with everything, which I expected and totally understood. She was really timid and careful when she walked, especially inside the house. Walking across the unfamiliar surface of the floor, she was very reticent and took slow, ordered steps, feeling her way from one spot to the next. She would pull her whole body back with each step, before putting her paw out in front to move forwards. Her body language spoke volumes about how difficult it must have been being blind and not knowing her way around, but I felt gladder than ever that she had a safe home now.

She walked like that all the time at first, but I was confident that in time she would become much more assured. I knew that a Kasey training regime would help her beat her insecurities and become the best, most confident version of herself!

Maggie walked around the flat with her head down really low so that she could smell everything and "sense" her way around. But once she learnt the layout of each room she gradually began picking her head up, and in remarkably little time she had worked out how to find her way without bumping into things. It was pretty incredible to watch.

I observed her a lot in that first week. I knew from experience that the best thing I could do was to have as little interaction with her as possible and give her the space she needed to settle in. Everything was new to her and I didn't want to make a fuss or give her a reason to worry. The calmer you are and the more you act like things are fine, the more a dog will think they are fine too. They pick up on how we're feeling in an instant, so I kept my own movements slow and measured, and gave her plenty of space when she had her dinner.

Each time you put water down for a blind dog you show them where it is, and you put it in the same place every time so they always know where to go. I did the same with her food – though being a bit on the greedy side, Maggie didn't have much of a problem finding that.

I didn't properly stroke her for about three days at the start, because I felt it was so important to give her space. I desperately wanted to meet her needs and allow her to do things at her own pace. I even used a loop lead so I didn't have to touch her.

Because I put her needs first, by the end of the first week I think she started to work things out for herself. "Okay, this lady means walks. Okay, this lady means food. Okay, maybe this lady isn't so bad after all." For Maggie, this was a crucial first step towards gaining the independence her blindness had threatened to take away.

I could tell when she was just having a lazy lie-down as opposed to sleeping, because her eyes and nose would still follow me around the room. Because the muscles in her left eye still worked, they would twitch if she was trying to keep a look out for me. The infection in her right eye must have been really bad, because she had no movement in that one. But she could still move her left eye and try to blink as if it still worked.

Maggie hadn't walked on a pavement for a year before she came to the UK, so the pads on her paws were thickened and calloused, making it difficult for her to walk on hard surfaces. It would be a difficult obstacle to overcome, but she wasn't going to let anything hold her back. She had a wider fear of being on different surfaces: it took a little while for her to readjust going from carpet to tiles, and I could see her trying to figure out where she was. Because her whole world was based only on what she could hear, smell, touch with her whiskers, or touch with her feet, she could easily get confused.

I took her down to the beach one day, and as all the beaches around Brighton are pebbled, she found it super weird. I thought she would love the new smells and sensations because all dogs seem to love frolicking around by the sea. But I think that because the stones were so uneven and unpredictable and there were so many ups and downs, she felt out of her depth, so we didn't last long on the rocks. It was too much too soon.

I needed to make sure she was adaptable to any form or surface, so after our first few walks I bought a big hay bale from a farm shop. I broke it up and sprinkled it on the floor of the field I was renting for my doggie day-care, and I hid treats in it to encourage her to walk around on it. I wanted to introduce her to weird sensations so that eventually nothing felt weird to her.

I also took her to really muddy areas so she got used to the sensation of her paws sinking into the ground, and I let her dip her paws into streams, but I constantly reassured her that she was okay. Again, I used treats to keep her moving. I've got a video of the first time she walked across a stream on her own, and it was so emotional. I was standing on the other side rustling a bag of treats, and I could see her thinking, "No, I can't do it, there's water!" Then, very slowly but surely, she walked across on her own and I shouted, "Go Maggie! Well done!" at the top of my voice.

It hadn't taken long for me to figure out that food was the key to training Maggie. Using treats as an incentive while training dogs is a great thing if you're using them in the right way. If you give a dog treats when it's fearful and stagnant to try and cheer it up or get them to do something, you're rewarding fearful behaviour, which isn't great. But guiding dogs with treats and encouraging them to do things, or rewarding them when they overcome a fear or learn a command, is a really positive thing.

The first time Maggie experienced sand, she really didn't know what to make of it. I guess the sensation is kind of like mud, but the grainy bits got clogged in her paws. And the sea was another challenge altogether.

I was still concerned about Maggie's physical well-being, as I hadn't yet got to the bottom of the funny little lump I'd found in her neck on her first day with me. When I took Maggie to the vet to get her checked up, the vet seemed equally unsure. He speculated that the lump was probably a result of broken cartilage where her ear had been cut off, but advised me to keep an eye on it. I felt reassured that it wasn't anything critical, but was still uneasy at how little I truly knew of Maggie's injuries and the discomfort they could potentially cause her. She seemed to have occasional pain in her legs and her jaw especially, and I was desperate to ensure she felt looked after. Although Maggie seemed to be doing well and didn't seem overly affected by her injuries, I knew we hadn't seen the last of them.

During those early days, I had to keep Maggie and Mishka in separate rooms most of the time, because every time Mishka wandered over to where Maggie was, Maggie would let out a really deep growl. And her growl was surprisingly fierce. I couldn't even feed them in the same room because having been a street dog, Maggie was so protective of her food. I think Maggie must have been more fearful of hyper Mishka than she initially let on, and they were very wary of each other to begin with. Mishka has a really authoritative energy, and I don't think Maggie knew how to cope with the challenge of another dog being in such close quarters.

Of course, Mishka was used to being around other dogs because of my day-care work, so she was really good at picking up on Maggie's signals and giving her space. But I could see that there were times where she was uncomfortable with her growling.

Growling is the last thing that dogs will do before they attack or bite. They're basically saying to you, "I don't like this, and if you carry on the way you are I am going to lash out." So it was difficult hearing it from Maggie, but equally I felt it was an important signal that I needed to pay attention to.

I never punish growling in the dogs I look after, because there's always a reason behind it. I would much rather fix the situation so that things are better going forward. That's how I've always trained my dogs. If a dog is so unnerved it's growling, it means you've done something wrong, so you need to fix that before it becomes aggressive. I always try to step back and look at what has happened to make the dog growl in the first place.

Mishka is quick to say when she wants her own space, and she is very tuned into knowing what she wants. Her verbal cues are more like a fox. Dogs are very clear with their signals and you can read their eyes or the way their ears move, but Mishka goes down low like a fox when she's angry, and sometimes she has delayed reactions.

If one dog comes up to another dog and it's uncomfortable, you would be able to tell from the messages it gives out. But it's hard to read Mishka. She can go from happy-go-lucky to "get the hell away from me" in two seconds flat. She doesn't really give out clear warnings. She's quite jittery and she's got a real hunter instinct – she's always on alert. Her tail is always flutter-ing, and whenever I see foxes on wildlife programmes I see similar traits in them.

The Maggie-Mishka situation was like when an only child gets a new brother or sister. Mishka was jealous. I've heard stories of children asking when the new baby is going back, because they don't like all the attention they're getting. It must be hard to go from having all the attention to having to share it with another child. Or in the case of Mishka, yet another dog.

So I had to be careful how I managed my interactions with both of them. If Maggie came over to me for a cuddle, I would always make sure I made a lot of fuss of Mishka afterwards. Maggie could also be quite jealous, but because she was blind she couldn't see me giving Mishka love. That probably made the settling in process that little bit easier. But for Mishka, it was a difficult adjustment.

Bit by bit, I made them more comfortable with the idea of spending long periods in the same room, but they were never very close to each other. If Maggie sat on the couch, Mishka would be on the floor, and if Maggie climbed down and sat on the floor, Mishka would get up on the couch. They didn't cuddle up to each other, and I had to make sure that I shared the love out because I could always tell when Mishka was feeling jealous of me giving Maggie attention.

Dogs often show anxiety by licking their lips or yawning. When Mishka was uncomfortable with something Maggie was doing, she'd show it by licking her lips. The problem, of course, was that Maggie couldn't see her do it. So Mishka would give a little growl, and if Maggie still didn't get the message she'd growl more loudly. Or if Mishka felt too stressed she'd just go and hide to get away from Maggie.

It wasn't Maggie's fault; she just didn't know any better and she hadn't been taught how she should act around other dogs. I could see Maggie growing surer of herself every day, and she had clearly started to really like Mishka, so she wanted to hang out with her more and more. The first time they played together was an amazing moment, but I had to watch them at all times. Maggie played quite rough and Mishka wasn't totally comfortable with it. She gave Maggie all the usual signals to tell her to back off, but because Maggie couldn't see them she carried on. A lot of it stemmed from excitement, but I was wary of the fact that I needed to keep socialising her bit by bit, gently and steadily, so she could start interacting with other dogs in a more relaxed fashion. Dogs use visual cues to signal their intentions when playing, and because Maggie couldn't see them, it made it all the more important to keep an eye on her when she was in company.

Maggie and Mishka did start to hang out together more as the weeks went on. It followed a pattern where Mishka would be playing happily with her, and then Maggie would get a little rough and Mishka would become scared. But once Mishka worked out that she could jump up on the bed or the couch to get away if she needed to, and poor Maggie wouldn't be able to see where she was, she felt much more secure. It took some of that fear away.

The problem was that as time went on, Maggie began to work out Mishka's safe places. She knew that if Mishka wasn't on the floor, she would be up high trying to get some time to herself. So as Maggie's confidence grew and she began to find her way around better, she would jump up to all the places she thought Mishka might be hiding, to try and find her.

Maggie's life is like one massive game of hide and seek, and she's really good at it. Before long even I couldn't resist getting involved, and I started hiding from Maggie and getting her to try and find me. I suppose that was what she was doing anyway, every single day.

But because she couldn't see, Maggie's other senses were sharp as anything. Her hearing in particular was on another level – despite the fact she only had one ear. It was remarkable to watch. A human can't hear sounds that vibrate at more than 20,000 vibrations per second, but dogs can up to 50,000 vibrations a second, so even with one-eared Maggie still had better hearing than me. Dogs are literally on a different frequency.

But Maggie's hearing was even better than two-eared Mishka's. I sometimes put an egg in the dogs' dinner, and Maggie knew if I was cracking an egg and got extra excited about it. And she was always at the window the second she heard my car, because she knew the sound of the engine. When Mishka was home alone, I could often sneak up to her and surprise her because she couldn't tell the sound of my car apart from other cars. But I could never get away with that with Maggie. I felt sure she'd be at the door waiting for me to arrive when I was still several streets away!

Because of her sensitive hearing, she was initially scared of Mishka's howling habit –perfectly naturally, I suppose. She must have thought it was a show of aggression, when it really wasn't. Mishka howls when she's excited, which seemed totally alien to Maggie at first. But once they began to get more used to each other's strange foibles, things started to really come together.

Maggie and Mishka progressed so well over the following weeks that eventually I began walking them together off the lead, and they would happily trot along together. And one day, I took the bold step of putting them both in the front of the van together while I collected one of my day-care dogs. When I came back to the van, Maggie and Mishka were sat down, all snuggled up together. It was like something out of a romantic film, and I couldn't help shedding a tear at the lovely sight. It was such a seismic moment in their relationship that I even remember the date – it was 29 September 2018. That was the first time they had ever snuggled together. And it was also the moment when I realised that perhaps I really could adopt Maggie if things continued in the right direction. Just because the dogs had a snuggle didn't mean that everything was going to be easy – I still had to keep a beady eye on them – but it was a massive step forward.

The Instagram message I posted six weeks after Maggie arrived sums up my feelings perfectly:

Maggie and Mishka did not hit it off to start with. Being completely blind and in a foreign environment, Maggie used to growl whenever she met a dog, even ones she knew. It wasn't that she was mean — it was simply a defence mechanism she had developed to protect herself as she couldn't read the other dog's body language. This led to a bit of fear in both dogs. A lot of supervised interactions and a quite a few bonding activities have really helped build their relationship. 6 weeks later they enjoy each other's company and have the odd play together. They eat in the same room, but I doubt I will ever trust them together with high-reward objects like bones and chews. It's slow progress every day, but it's so rewarding to see them so happy together.

CHAPTER SIX
MORE ABOUT MISHKA

So, what about magnificent Mishka – how did she end up coming to live with me?

It's definitely not as dramatic as Maggie's story, but we know Mishka can get a little jealous, so it wouldn't be fair on her if she didn't have her own little *tail* to tell.

When I first started my day-care business three years ago, I went through a little period feeling quite lonely. When you're starting a business you have to put all your time and effort and money into that, and I felt like I wasn't seeing my friends very much. It was just work, work, work, and all I wanted to do was build up my business so that I had a good foundation for my future. But that became quite isolating and there were times when I felt really down.

It's true that a dog can't really talk back and have a proper conversation with you – as much as they would love to. But they can offer real companionship, love and trust. And looking after so many wonderful dogs on a daily basis made me realise that what I was really missing was a dog of my own, who I could spend time with both during and after work. And I knew there were dogs out there in need of a safe, loving home.

So I decided to register to foster a dog. I filled out an application form online saying that I would happily take a rescue if one came up, thinking it would probably never happen. But several months, later I got an email explaining that an opportunity had come up, and was I interested in fostering an Alaskan Klee Klai?

They explained her issues and told me her story. She had been bought by a lady who very soon afterwards got a job working abroad, so Mishka was passed on to another person to look after.

However, her mum was already overstretched because she was looking after an unwell family member while running a business, and she also had five dogs of her own. Because of that, Mishka's only interaction with other pooches was being constantly told off by four older dogs. I can imagine Mishka was a very bouncy puppy, so to minimise her contact with the other dogs she was kept in a crate for most of the day. She had shock collars put on her, and even now it's hard to put a collar or harness on because she's afraid in case it's going to hurt her. On top of that, she was muzzled because she used to jump up and lunge at people. She was very territorial – a little fireball.

I'm not against muzzles at all, because some dogs need them if they're aggressive, or if they eat things they shouldn't when they're out for walks. But Mishka's muzzle was put on just to stop her barking. This was deeply unfair, because barking is a part of a puppy's learning. Barking is a natural instinct, and if it gets too much you need to step in and do some training. But you do not stick a muzzle on a dog and hope that it learns to shut up. It doesn't work like that. That will do more harm than good, because then the puppy won't be able to express itself at all and it will probably wind up even more stressed and agitated. Naturally, it will then want to bark even more once the muzzle is removed. So I knew just from reading about her that Mishka had had a rough time of it, but that certainly didn't scare me off.

The first time I ever met Mishka was at her former owner's house in June 2018. She had the shock collar and muzzle on, and it was clear she hadn't had any training.

She came running over to me and she was jumping up and growling, but I didn't mind about any of that. I knew some people would be put off by a dog behaving so boisterously, but I could see that her reaction was just a mixture of fear and excitement, and she wasn't a bad dog in the slightest. I loved her immediately, and so what if she had some behavioural issues that needed ironing out? Challenge accepted!

Mishka is a funny old dog. She looks a bit like a wolf and behaves like a fox. She's a small girl, just like Maggie. Small dogs suit my lifestyle because I take my dogs everywhere I go. I felt like this could just be the perfect fit.

I took Mishka for a walk around the garden, took her muzzle off and gave her some treats. I could see instantly how calm and loving she was capable of being. She just hadn't been given a chance before. I knew Mishka hadn't been out for a proper walk in a long time, and that was the reason she was always hyper. Apparently, she often used to jump the fence to try and escape, or try and burrow her way into the neighbouring fields, and I think that was because she was bored and had so much pent-up energy. I knew I just needed to give her time and patience.

I felt confident I could help Mishka if we spent some proper time together. She would have the chance to train, socialise and play in a way she hadn't before. So I decided I could foster Mishka for a year or so, and then once I had helped her become a happier, more sociable dog, she could go to a forever home. I was enormously excited by the prospect of having such a lovely dog in my life, and I offered to take her in on the spot.

Mishka's owners wanted to think things over that night and make sure they were doing the right thing, so I had a very long, agonising wait wondering if I would be able to foster her. I couldn't concentrate on anything, and I must have phoned my mum five times at work to ask her if she thought everything was going to be okay. I was desperate for her to come and live with me.

I finally got a call the next morning confirming that Mishka's current owners were happy for me to foster her. I was elated, and rushed over there straight away. When I arrived I gave her the biggest hug (I won't lie, she seemed pretty nonplussed) and then I led her to my van.

I knew I could transform Mishka into a loving and eager-to-please pup, but she had some serious issues in the early days. I had already pre-arranged to do doggy day-care for Lolli and Lennard, and I knew Lolli would be perfect for Mishka to go on her first walk with, because she's so good with other dogs. I also confirmed that Lolli and Lennard's owner was okay with me walking them all together.

I took the three of them to Devil's Dyke in Brighton, because it's very open and there's tons of space, but Mishka's issues became very apparent the moment I went to take her out of the van. As soon as I opened the door, she backed away and growled at me. It wasn't the best start, but I got it. She still didn't really know who I was and she was scared, just as anyone else would be if they were approached by a stranger.

I kept Mishka's muzzle on until I was sure she wouldn't be aggressive towards the other two. At that point I had no idea about the extent of her fear of other dogs, so it was better to be safe than sorry.

She was brilliant on the walk, and she didn't react to any of the other dogs we saw. I think having Lolli by her side really helped – Lolli is always a reassuring presence among the dogs I look after.

Two hours later, she was so tired out that I'm not sure she had it in her to growl. As soon as she went into her crate she fell into a deep sleep.

I knew the main thing I had to do with Mishka was to socialise her more, which involved me taking her to lots of parks. One day we met a woman who was walking her dog, and her dog and Mishka got on so well that they were soon running around having the time of their lives.

I started meeting the same woman every day for walks, and seeing Mishka playing with her dog was such a breath of fresh air. For the first time, she seemed totally happy and carefree. It was also a helpful way of introducing Mishka to people when she was feeling relaxed. Meeting people is unavoidable when you're in a busy park, so she just had to get on with it. Her real motivation was going to see her doggie friend every day, and that meant she had to be around a lot of human beings too. It all helped to de-sensitise her when she had previously been so jumpy and anxious. She was still nervous of other people, but I would ask random strangers in the park to give her a biscuit so she started trusting humans more. I knew it would take a while, just as it would take some time for me to build up real trust with Mishka.

She wasn't aggressive towards people as such, but she was scared. If there was a situation that unnerved her, she would take herself away rather than go on the attack. But if she was on the lead and she felt like she was trapped or cornered, she would growl and I would have to get her to somewhere she felt safe.

I never imagined that she would end up being a sociable and calm dog as such. I knew that her breed is often quite socially aloof, so she wasn't ever going to be like a friendly Labrador who smothers strangers with affection, but that was fine with me. I knew what I had taken on, and I loved her as she was.

I put in a lot of hours socialising Mishka, and after a few months it got to a point where a stranger could come up and stroke her and she wouldn't react. She's such a beautiful looking dog that people have always been interested in her and want to say hello. I was still mindful of her problems, and I would always warn people in advance that she was quite nervous, but after a while I no longer had to worry about her growling or barking. The Kasey regime was working!

Mishka might be cute and small (she only weighs 11kg!), but I knew not to be fooled. She is a squirrel-hunting machine. I don't think she'll ever actually catch one, but I don't like to mention it to her. Mishka is also totally fearless around other dogs. In her head, she's large and in charge, and she'll put any pooch in its place.

She developed a rather questionable habit of stealing plastic bottles out of the recycling bin and chewing them up in the garden. She had all these lovely toys to play with, but no, she wanted an empty water bottle to go to town on instead. I also quickly realised that she was a prolific poo roller. It was like anything smelly and disgusting held some kind of magnetism for her. If I didn't catch her in time, she'd be rolling on her back in it in no time at all, smiling up at the sun like she was in heaven.

I hate to tell tales, but she also has a peculiar taste cow pats, and has a very rude habit of sticking her nose in people's crotches when she meets them. Could there be any less pleasant greeting?

But I could see Mishka was becoming a happy ball of energy, ever readier for adventure and trying out new things. I knew from the start how intelligent she was – she could learn a new trick in minutes, and loved showing them off once she'd mastered them. She was also evidently incredibly loyal and would walk to the ends of the earth if I asked her to.

And I could swear Mishka could read my mind. Even if I just thought about taking her out for a walk, she'd be at the front door, raring to go. A sleeping Maggie, by contrast, will often have to be coerced out of bed, especially if the weather isn't great.

Mishka is a real success story, though it is important to consider the amount of work that was needed to integrate her into normal life. I made it my job to improve Mishka's behavioural problems to the point where she could be rehomed on a permanent basis, but if she had been rehomed before I had done that, she might never have got over those problems. Many well-intentioned people are happy to take on a rescue dog, but they can't always put in the hours of intensive training and careful socialisation that is needed. That's where us foster carers come in. If foster carers put in the work to help iron out a dog's issues, it gives the dog a much greater chance of a happy and healthy life. I felt I had done a good job with her, and she had responded wonderfully.

Needless to say, I soon realised that I'd totally fallen in love with Mishka. I was kidding myself if I thought I was going to pass her on for rehoming. I knew that I could never let her go, and once that realisation hit, that was it. I knew that keeping her was the only option, and that was one of the best decisions I've ever made.

CHAPTER SEVEN
THE TRIALS AND TRIBULATIONS OF TRAINING

When I first got Maggie she would often growl at Mishka, and she could go from being calm to being really angry very quickly. There was nothing in between, and no real warning signs. I think she was more distressed than anything else, but it was like she went from 0 to 100, which was very confusing for Mishka, who wouldn't know what she'd done wrong.

Maggie used to bark a lot too, but that quickly calmed down. While she was on the streets she must have had to be on constant alert, and she was probably always on the defensive, waiting for the next bad thing to happen. Now she was safe, but it was a real learning curve for her to trust humans and animals again.

You might think it would have been frightening for Maggie when she was first brought over to the UK, because she was leaving everything she had known behind. But if anything, I think it helped that things were so different. It was a fresh start, which was probably exactly what she needed. She even had to try and understand a totally new-sounding language.

She had only heard people speaking Arabic, so it must have been very confusing for her hearing English. And obviously, it was even harder because she couldn't follow visual signals either, so she would have to learn words in a new language in order to be able to understand commands. Nowadays she's tri-lingual – she speaks English, Arabic and Dog.

But Maggie was a quick learner. When she wanted. Funnily enough, she learnt "treats" and "dinner" in no time at all. But amazingly, even after all this time, sometimes she still doesn't understand the word "no".

I was wary of exposing her to people while we were out and about, because of her traumatic past. Much like Mishka, having suffered such cruel abuse, it was unlikely she'd willingly trust strangers at first. I was aware that some dogs react to the strangest things, whether it's small children or high-visibility jackets, because they associate them with bad things that happened to them in the past. I knew a rescue dog who was really friendly and lovely with everyone, but used to go crazy at the postman. His owners couldn't understand it, until they were walking with him in a town centre and he barked at two people who were wearing Dr Martens boots. They realised that the boots were identical to the ones their postman wore, and that was possibly the cause of the dog's defensive response. It could have been that he was abused by someone who wore similar boots, and that he would always link them with his past experiences.

So it might sound crazy to say that there are bonuses to Maggie being blind, but if you think about it, if she were to see someone who looked like one of her cruel attackers, she would freak out. Perhaps it's a blessing that she's oblivious to how anyone looks. People think Maggie is disadvantaged, but I think in some ways she's advantaged because she can't see things that would make other dogs fearful.

But in the early days she did have a couple of surprising reactions to people in the street. The first time it happened, we were in a park and she ran off and hid in a bush and refused to come out, which isn't like her at all. There weren't any other noises that could have freaked her out, so I couldn't understand it. I thought she was just having a bit of a crazy moment. All that I noticed was a strong smell of aftershave from a man who had just walked past.

The second time, we were walking down the street and a man came over to say hello to Maggie. She jumped back from him and tried to run away. Again, the man's aftershave was so strong it made me want to cough. That was the only connection I could make between the two episodes, so I concluded that perhaps one of her abusers used to drown himself in cheap cologne.

Sensations, sights, smells and sounds stay with dogs, and unless it's trained out of them, those issues can last a lifetime. You can't get a rescue dog and expect it to be perfect, but they can be trained with a lot of love and attention. And if you take on a rescue dog, you have to be willing to put in the work to make that happen. It's not fair to take on a dog and then send it back to the rescue shelter if it doesn't instantly behave impeccably. You have to understand that the dog has already been through a lot, and it's only going to confuse them further if they're shunted from home to home.

Maggie had issues with some sounds, which took a lot of training to work past. Having been a street dog for so long, she was used to loud noises, but she didn't like anything outside her comfort zone. I remember dropping and smashing a plate about two months after I got her and she didn't even react. But if a lorry went past when we were walking through Brighton, she would freak out. Lorries, buses and boy racers frightened her. She would instantly panic and start turning around in circles. She was so scared on one occasion that she slipped her collar and tried to run away. I managed to grab her, but I thought I was going to pass out because I was so shaken up. Whatever it was, something about the noise and the motion of loud cars really triggered her.

I began to wonder whether she had been hit by a car when she was living on the streets. It was heartbreaking trying to piece together the missing parts of her story, but I felt it was fundamental in trying to understand her experiences and associations as much as possible in order to train her to cope with them better.

Because Maggie only had one ear, collars weren't as secure on her as they are on other dogs, which made it easier for her to slip out of them and run away if she was scared. Once she learnt that she could navigate her way out, I had to come up with a plan B to ensure we could go for safe, stress-free walks. I tried to use a harness on her, but because she was still a little overweight, it chafed her nipples and made her feel uncomfortable. And if a dog is nervous and uncomfortable, they're even less likely to want to walk.

In the end I had to switch to a slip lead for a while, a type of lead that tightens around the dog if they try to run away, and that is often used for training dogs. I had to do it for her safety. It just tightened a little bit if Maggie tried to slip it. I only ever put it on her when we were in built-up places where she might be spooked, and then if a lorry or motorbike passed I would hold her close to me and give her a treat to reinforce the notion that there was nothing to be afraid of.

I felt like Maggie and I were developing an amazing level of communication. We kind of "got" each other, and I would never make her do anything I didn't think she was comfortable with. I would definitely sense if there was something she wasn't keen on, and I would never put her into a situation where I knew she wouldn't be okay.

Traffic is a part of everyday life and it's unavoidable, so I had no choice but to get her used to it. If she did freak out if a bus came along, the best thing I could do was act as normally as possible and keep moving.

Meanwhile, when we were at home I started a course of desensitisation training for Maggie, as I have done for each dog I've fostered, playing videos of various noises on YouTube to get the dogs used to them. I started playing the sounds of traffic really quietly in the background every time she had breakfast or dinner, so she began to make positive associations with the noise. In her mind, the sound of traffic soon became like a dinner bell, and she deduced that scary traffic noises actually meant she was getting food.

Every week, I began turning the volume up a little bit because Maggie responded well, but if a dog is really fearful, it's best just to do it once every two weeks. It's a very measured method and it doesn't get overnight results, but it does work eventually.

Eventually she reached the point where she might stop in her tracks if a boy racer tore past, but she wouldn't freak out or spin around and try to get away.

A lot of dogs have huge issues with fireworks, and you would expect Maggie to be terrified of them because they sound so much like gunshots. But she didn't seem bothered by them one bit. On Bonfire Night, she went out for a wee while fireworks popped all around her and she didn't even seem to notice. Again, I think I had my desensitisation training to thank.

It's a case of keeping it up, but I would advise anyone who has a dog that reacts to fireworks to play the noises in the background for several months before Bonfire Night. I promise you, you will see a change in your dog.

When I first got Maggie, I treated her very differently from how I treated Mishka when she came to live with me. Because she didn't know where she was, I picked Maggie up and put her down every time she needed to move. If she needed to get up onto the sofa or get into the van I would help her, and she was very willing to be pampered. I assumed she would always need additional support.

But then one day she surprised me. I sat her down next to the van while I put Mishka in the passenger seat, and suddenly Mags jumped from the pavement into the footwell and then hopped up onto the front seat next to Mishka. I was stunned! It certainly wasn't something I'd taught her to do, and I had no idea how she'd learnt it.

A lot of dog training is done using sight and eye contact. Needless to say I couldn't do that with Maggie, so I used repetition instead. Once I knew she could jump into the van, I started to pat the seat and say "shotgun", and she would jump right in. If she was going in the back with the other dogs, I'd say to her "paws up", and she knew she needed to jump up and wait for me to put her into a crate.

When I wanted her to jump up onto something I'd say "paws" and then tap it, and she'd hop right up and wait for her treat. She also learned to sit on command, although sometimes she liked to pretend she hadn't heard me if she couldn't be bothered.

Getting her to walk perfectly on a lead wasn't one of my top priorities, because there were so many other things to overcome first, but once she did get used to walking on a lead she was amazing. She took to it so quickly.

Walking a blind dog is a tricky business, so as soon as she'd mastered the lead, I started teaching her left and right, by tugging on her lead lightly and pulling her to the right, saying "right", or pulling her to the left, saying (you guessed it!) "left". Once she had learnt those commands, I tried using the same commands with her off the lead. She got the hang of it instantly. I was absolutely delighted.

If I ever thought she was going to bump into something I would say, "Maggie, watch!" and that soon became her stop command. As soon as I said, "Watch, watch, watch!" she knew it was serious! Her responsiveness continued to astonish me with every passing day.

The first time she had to go up a flight of wooden steps she was really nervous, and I had to get the really good treats out for that because she was worried about slipping. She did it in the end, bless her heart, but I knew I had to train her to be able to manage for herself.

So I taught her to walk upstairs by saying "step up" when she got to the bottom of a flight of stairs. She would put her paw out in front of her and feel around for the stair or ledge. She then used her nose to feel for the next step, so I didn't have to repeat "step up" over and over again. Maggie was swiftly proving herself a smart girl, and she automatically knew to feel her way, using her nose and whiskers to find out if there was another step coming up. She did the same thing coming down, and leaning forward and brushing her whiskers around to see if there was another step beneath her. When she got to the top or bottom of a flight of stairs she would feel around, and if there wasn't another step she knew it was safe to walk on. She is so good at it now I don't have to think about it, but when we first started I was always worried that she was going to stumble.

When we were out walking in the woods and a tree had fallen down or there was a big log blocking our path, I'd say, "Step up," and she knew there was something in her way that she needed to step over.

Maggie loved going on walks, but she did often hang back with me. She was a bit of a mummy's girl. Mishka would run ahead, going crazy with all the other dogs, but Maggie didn't really like the chaos of it all.

But Maggie became braver as time went on. If we were going for a walk in a place she knew well, sometimes she'd take herself off to investigate an interesting scent or sound. Once she'd learnt all the twists and turns, she naturally started taking herself out of her comfort zone, and it was great to see her discover new things.

We went for regular walks in the woods and she did bump her head on a good few trees, but it never seemed to affect her, and it was great to see her adventurous spirit coming out. Given that any kind of walk was a struggle when I first put her on the lead, it really was like witnessing a miracle in real time. I used to have to carry her when she got tired, but soon she took to walking for hours.

And she loved nothing more than going for a walk along the beach. She sniffed out all sorts of things, from seagull feathers to empty shells, and always seemed fascinated with every new thing she came across. I felt so proud seeing how inquisitive she was becoming. She didn't go swimming in the sea, but she didn't mind if the waves came up and lapped her paws. Mishka was a bit braver and would go in until the water came up to her belly, and she'd splash about a bit, but she wouldn't go full-on swimming.

I quickly learnt that two of Maggie's favourite smells were salty air and other people's food, so she usually spent most of our seaside visits with her nose high in the air, taking it all in. One of Maggie's favourite places to go, combining both food and the smell of the sea, is the Big Beach Cafe on the Lagoon in Hove. It's a really cute cafe, and they are big dog lovers in there, and if you know the secret passcode ("Please can I have a doggy sausage") they'll reach underneath the counter into the fridge and produce a chilled sausage for your dog to savour.

I had seen so many dogs pull their owners all the way to the counter, and sometimes dogs would dart away from their owners and be found sat in the cafe, waiting for a spare sausage to magically appear. Maggie was no different. As soon as she realised where she was, she would weave her way up to the counter and give them her best "feed me" look. Once she'd had her sausage it was straight down to the beach, where she liked to strip off her collar or banana and run free.

She was also growing more confident around people she didn't know and in unfamiliar houses. Before long, she could go into any house and instinctively know where things like tables and sofas were. And, needless to say, she could always sniff out a toy box if the owners of the house had a dog.

She would still bump her head every now and again, but those occasions were getting rarer and rarer, and she got used to the odd knock, so it stopped fazing her. She amazed me in those first few months. I would look at her and think, "Imagine if you did have your sight, Maggie. What would you be doing then?" She could have taken on the world. In a way, that was exactly what she was doing.

The final thing I had to master was Maggie's habit of jumping up at people. It might have seemed cute and friendly – but I knew she only did it when she knew there was food around. She may have thought she was being subtle, but I could see right through her. She would stand up on her hind legs and wave her paws to let the person know she wanted to eat.

I had been careful about Maggie's diet from day one, especially as she needed to lose weight. I'm not a vet or nutritionist, but I want my dogs to live a long life. There's a huge movement to feed your dogs raw food, and I read that if you fed your dogs kibble, adding vegetables to your dogs' diet, they could live for up to two years longer. There was a study done on 100 dogs that were fed kibble, and 100 dogs that were fed kibble with vegetables, and the dogs with added vegetables lived longer. People often think dogs are carnivores, but they're omnivores – they eat both meat and vegetables.

I fed Maggie and Mishka kibble, because it has all the nutrients of a good diet, and I mixed it with different meats and vegetables. Some people have issues with their dog's digestion, but I never have, and I think that's because I feed my dogs pretty much everything. Some vets advise not changing up pets' diets too much, but I've found that by feeding them on a really varied diet, none of my dogs have ever had issues.

Each dog and each breed are different and there is a bit of controversy around what dogs should eat, but I generally go with what dogs would have eaten during their history with humans, which is basically what we eat if we're eating a healthy, balanced diet.

I'm sure dogs would not do well on all the fast food and processed rubbish we all enjoy from time to time. I would not feed my dogs a lot of human food, because of all the additives and processing in much of it these days. Dogs are also allergic to a lot of ingredients like onions, raisins and chocolate, so I'm super careful when I do give them my leftovers.

It is equally shocking how much sugar is in cheap dog food and biscuits. Dogs are just as addicted to sugar as we humans are, so no wonder they wolf all of that stuff down. We would probably like the biscuits too if we tried them. With all the added sugar, they probably don't taste much different to the ones we dip in our tea.

Maggie and Mishka did get plenty of great treats, it's true, but I tried to keep them as natural as possible. And that generally meant they smelt really, really bad. Why do dogs love the most disgusting chews you can get?

I soon found that my two were never happier than when they were chewing on a pig's foot. Take it from me, there are few things worse than the smell of a wet chewed pig's foot – well, apart from pizzle sticks (which are, ahem, dried bull's penises). Not surprisingly, they smelt grotesque. Those and sprats, which are little reeking dried fish, soon became Maggie's favourites.

Sprats smell like nothing else on earth, but if I really wanted to reward Maggie, it was those stinky little buggers all the way. It was mortifying when we met new people just after the girls had been eating them, the stench seemed to be trying to escape from their very pores. The smell lingered for so long that if Maggie jumped up and licked someone, they would probably run a three-minute mile to get to the nearest sink. And she was always jumping up at people to try and get another treat.

She always wanted more food. So many street dogs don't know where the next meal is coming from, so needless to say they're going to try and eat as much as much as possible as often as they can in case they end up starving again. And Maggie was no different. She didn't mind whose food she was eating in order to do that.

Jumping up at people to be friendly is one thing, but jumping up at people to beg for food is a whole other ball game, and I had to train Maggie intensively to overcome the habit. Everything is auditory for Maggie, so the first whiff of food or the sound of a food package used to be such a trigger. Anytime I ate something she would have her nose in the air thinking it was for her.

She jumped up at my mum a lot, so every time she did it I would pull her off, make her sit, and then give her a treat. Eventually she learned that if she sat nicely, she would get a treat. Soon enough, any time I said sit, I could see her getting all excited because she thought she was going to get something delicious.

Everything was about repetition with Maggie. My mum, my sister and I always sat down for dinner in front of the TV, rather than sitting at a table. It was just what we'd always done. That was hell for Maggie, because the food was exactly at nose height. She was always coming up and trying to get our food because she was a street dog and she hadn't ever learnt any manners, and because she couldn't tell the difference between human food and dog food. All she knew was that it smelt good!

She had a little routine. At first, she would come and sit near you and act a little nonchalant. Then, slowly but surely, she would edge closer and closer so she was almost sitting on top of your plate. Believe me, there's nothing quite like the feeling of hot Maggie breath on your cutlery to put you off your food.

Every time she did it I kept telling her "no", and she would eventually walk away (she liked to pretend she couldn't hear very well out of her remaining ear, but eventually had to admit defeat). She would then move on to the next person who had food and stand in front of them until they shooed her away, so that method wasn't terribly successful.

She also used to make a soft little whimpering noise that melted my heart! It wasn't loud enough to drown out the TV, but just at the right pitch to make you feel like a terrible person for not sharing your meal with her.

So I began to move her away from the food and make her sit before giving her a treat. Over time she learned that she had *her* food and I had *my* food, and when I finished my dinner, if there was anything leftover that she and Mishka could share, then they got it – but they got it in their bowl.

I have never fed them off a plate. I think once you do that, it's really hard to go back. You can't feed your dog off the plate one day and then expect it not to try and do it again the following day. If you do it once, they think it's okay, and they don't understand that you're just doing it as a "treat". And you have to educate all the people around you, too. If your mum or your brother or your girlfriend feed them from their plates, they will think it's open season.

A lot of the food we eat is perfectly okay for dogs, and I believe that variety is the spice of life, so I'm happy to feed my dogs leftovers that are palatable for them. I'd rather that than just chucking it in the bin. But they know full well that if they're going to get anything, they're not going to get it while I'm eating. Neither Maggie or Mishka will ever come over to me when I'm eating now. It's like they don't notice and they don't beg.

Maggie would still jump up at people when she was super-excited, but the food side of things noticeably improved. I knew it wasn't fair to let my dog jump up at other people, because you never know who is a dog lover and who might be scared of them. In short, it was my responsibility and I had to own it. A lot of children can be fearful of dogs, so I had to have Maggie and Mishka under control at all times. You definitely have to toughen up when you get a dog.

I could have treated Maggie with kid gloves from day one and made sure she was on the lead all the time. I could have indulged her eating habits and kept her away from people and other dogs, but in the long term that probably would have made her problems worse.

Excitable dogs would continue to come crashing into her because they didn't understand that she couldn't see them, but I had to let them work it out between themselves. If I allowed myself to get nervous about it, Maggie would have picked up on that, and it would have made her even more nervous going forward. It was best for her to learn on her own how to deal with the chaos that is our life.

I've met a lot of dogs over the years and Maggie is very clever in a lot of ways, but it did take us around a year to get to a really good place with her training. I think that was partly because there was so much to learn, and partly because she's so stubborn. If she didn't want to do something, she wouldn't do it. Maggie is a renegade. She lives by her own rules.

Maggie was now visibly more comfortable around other dogs, but I found that she would play quite roughly with them. She didn't fully understand how to interact with house-trained dogs, being a bit of a streetfighter herself. So although she was beginning to settle in to social life, it was initially quite hard to find her friends to have fun with.

The first time Maggie played with another dog aside from Mishka, I knew she felt properly settled and was opening up. It was Hector the sausage dog, one of my day-care dogs, who decided Maggie was going to be his new BFF whether she liked it or not. It did take him a while to win her over, though.

When they first met, Hector was determined to make Maggie play, but at first her attitude was "talk to the paw". Hector spent days on end during dog-care sessions trying to get her on side. He was a one-pup mission to make her his mate.

One day he went over to lure her into a game of a chase (for about the hundredth time) and, to my huge surprise, she finally started playing with him. It was one of the most beautiful things I'd ever seen, and I took a video and sent it to everyone I knew.

And seeing them playing together was the funniest thing. Because Hector is short and Maggie can't see him, he could run away from her with ease. He'd dash away, do a full circle of the field where I looked after my day-care dogs, and then run back and slam his entire body into her, and she'd jump and start chasing him again. Those two could play wrestle for hours and hours, and he had absolutely no fear of Maggie whatsoever.

Devastatingly, Hector and his family moved away to Bristol around six months later. He had been Maggie's first proper playmate, and I knew how much she would miss him. Whenever he comes back and they meet up, they are so happy to see each other. If I say to her, "Where is Hector?" she'll start looking around for him. I'm convinced she thinks he's her boyfriend.

Maggie also made another sausage dog friend called Jeremy, though he was much more timid than Hector. I think he was a bit more fearful of getting hurt, because he's only small. Hector is quite a big sausage, because his grandad was a Labrador (work that one out) but Jeremy is quite little.

When Jeremy first started coming to day-care, you could see that he kind of wanted to join in the fun, but he was worried he might get stepped on. But he loved Maggie and would follow her around everywhere. It was like she was his bodyguard and she was protecting him. You could see him physically change when he was around her, and she treated him like he was her child.

He spent a lot of time with Maggie because they had similar personalities in some ways. When I first got her, if things felt too much, she would take herself off and spend some time on her own, and Jeremy was exactly the same. He loved people, but sometimes he just needed Jeremy time – he was very happy in his own company.

Jeremy came along to day-care every week and I really saw his confidence grow alongside Maggie's during that time. They really helped each other, and now they are both great with other dogs. Jeremy's only issue was that he liked to tell off puppies, which was a really common thing for adult dogs to do. Young pups are bouncy and yappy and unsocialised, and they have to learn from the older and (sometimes) wiser dogs, who feel like they need to put them in their place. It takes a village to raise a child and older dogs tell younger dogs off, just like adults tell off children.

As for Mishka, Maggie's development was helping her even more. Maggie was so friendly and so desperate to love, and as she became bolder, she would go straight up to people and demand that they notice her. And one-eared Maggie is such a cute little dog that people have always been only too willing to oblige. I think as a result of that, Mishka, who had been so scared of people for so long, began to understand even better that it's okay to say hello to people you don't know.

Besides, Mishka always wanted the same attention that Maggie got, so she started to emulate Maggie's behaviour to make sure she succeeded. It almost became a bit of a competition to see who could get the most affection from strangers. In that sense, Maggie really helped Mishka come out of her shell, which was a joy to see.

Quite often I would ask people to say hello to Maggie first, because once Mishka saw that Maggie was getting attention, she would get a bit jealous and decide to say hello too. Once she knew that Maggie was comfortable with somebody, that made her relax much more. All of a sudden, she was much more likely to go up and say hello to people and be friendly.

And Mishka was a brilliant help for Maggie's growth and development too. I don't think Maggie would be the same dog as she is if I hadn't already had Mishka, who is so active. Given the chance, I think Maggie would have carried on being a couch potato like she had been in her previous home. But being around Mishka encouraged her to go out and meet people and other dogs.

Maggie and Mishka were getting along better and better. Mishka sometimes liked to pinch Maggie's toys, and Maggie would sometimes nick her bones. But if either of them ever got upset, I would tell the other one to back off, and they instantly would. It was never a serious problem. I think they quickly developed a lot of respect for each other. And if they did tell each other off, it felt healthy. That was how they learned each other's boundaries.

Toys were a funny prospect for Maggie at first. At first, she really didn't take to squeaky toys at all. If I offered her one and squeaked it under her nose, she would back away. If she ever picked up a squeaky toy by mistake and it made a noise, she would instantly freeze and drop the toy. I think there are probably a few reasons for that.

I think one reason was that, being a street dog, she'd never had a squeaky toy before, so she didn't really understand what it was. To her, it was just a lump of plastic that made a weird noise. And another reason could have been that, to her, maybe it sounded like a dog sounds when it's in pain.

I also wondered if she thought it was me who was hurt. In the early days when Maggie played with me, she used to bite quite hard. She didn't ever mean to hurt me, but because she hadn't been taught how to playfight with people, she had no inhibitions. I had to teach her that it hurt me if she bit too hard, because humans are much more sensitive than dogs. Human nerve endings are much higher up in our skin than dogs' are. Theirs are kind of hidden, which is why they're able to play so roughly without hurting each other.

Because I couldn't show Maggie that I was uncomfortable visually, I used to make a squealing noise so that she knew she was being too boisterous. I think it must have sounded a bit too similar to a squeaky toy, so it was hard for her to differentiate.

The good thing was that Mishka is a massive fan of squeaky toys and was constantly squeaking them in Maggie's ear, so she had no choice but to get used to the sound. They still weren't her favourite thing – she gradually got over her fear of them – but she stopped overreacting when Mishka was trying to rip one in half.

Being such a softie at heart, Maggie preferred cuddly dog toys. When I gave her one, she would always show her appreciation by instantly ripping off the ears and the eyes. I reckoned she was trying to make a Maggie teddy. But then the tail and legs would follow next, and soon there wouldn't be much left to play with. A lot of dogs are destructive with their toys, but Maggie had a real routine of how she liked to take them apart. Once the stuffing started to come out of the middle I had to throw them away, but I tried to let her enjoy them for as long as possible.

Nowadays the girls still have the odd blip, but they take it all in their stride and most of the time they adore each other. I really do think they see each other as sisters, and there is definitely a lot of love there.

CHAPTER EIGHT
MY STRANGE BEDFELLOW

When I told some people that I was fostering Maggie, not everyone was positive. On hearing about her injuries, some people said in a very gentle way, "Would it not be better for her if…"

Knowing Maggie as well as I did, it would be easy for me to respond with anger and outrage. But as someone who has spent so long caring for dogs, I understood their concerns about her wellbeing and quality of life. But my thinking was that if the vets out in Lebanon deemed her worthy of surviving in an environment as harsh as it can be there, Maggie was clearly going to be capable or surviving here, where she was going to be loved and cared for.

Besides, Maggie was growing a lot stronger in every way. When I first started taking her out for walks, she would get tired out so quickly. Because she'd been lying down for so long in the rescue home in Lebanon, she didn't have much muscle mass any more. She was significantly overweight after spending three months sitting on a sofa barely moving. She clearly felt weak and exhausted doing the smallest things, because her body had got out of the habit of moving around. With regular exercise and good food, I got her back to a normal weight of 15 kg, spot on for a dog of her height. I had been worried Maggie would be left with a lot of loose skin once she lost weight, but amazingly she snapped back into a really good shape (I sound like I work for a women's magazine!) I had to be careful with her, because like most dogs she adored food, and like most dogs she knew cunning ways to get it, which included giving you loads of love so you wanted to love her back. But I knew that if I showed love with food alone, I wouldn't be doing Maggie any favours.

It was as she lost weight, though, that I began to notice some strange things happening. One week, two little red marks appeared on her skin. They looked a little bit like insect bites, but they were concave, rather than bumpy. I had no idea where they'd come from, but thought they would probably disappear on their own if I left them alone for a few days.

Later that week I found two tiny little round things on the floor near where Maggie was lying. I picked them up, wondering where on earth they'd come from. They were hard to the touch, perfectly round and had a metallic feel.

I didn't put two and two together at the time, but when I checked Maggie's marks a few days later, they had got better again. The skin had levelled out and its redness wasn't quite so raw. I was utterly confused. As Maggie lost weight and became skinnier, I also noticed a bump on her forehead – another little flawless bump that felt perfectly round when I ran my finger over it. But as it was so small and Maggie didn't seem to be in pain when I touched it, I decided to think no more of it.

My concerns were abated by the fact that Maggie's mental condition was clearly improving enormously. She whimpered less in her sleep, and I began to hope that her nightmares were a thing of the past. When the doubters met her, I could see their thought patterns changing when they saw how capable she was.

Maggie had never been used to walking in woods and fields, another reason why walks tired her out so much at first. But after a few months of training I could take her out all day with me and she didn't get tired any more. If I went to meet a friend for a coffee, I took her and Mishka with me. Maggie might have a sit down once we were there, but most of the time she'd want to be up and about, seeing if there was anyone around who might like to stroke her.

As soon as I started taking Maggie for walks, people began stopping me to ask about her. It was hard to know what to say to people at times, because part of me was looking for a permanent home for her, and the other part of me was secretly hoping I might just be able to adopt her myself.

I would usually say to people, "She is the best dog ever. I'm just fostering her at the moment while we look for someone to adopt her. But I might adopt her!" I would always have to add the "but" in, just in case someone said, "I'll take her!" I wanted her to have the best home possible, and I wanted to be one of her options. I was terrified that someone would say to me, "We want her!" and the choice would be taken away from me.

The first thing people usually noticed about Maggie was that she was missing an ear, and they would ask what happened to it. Next, they would notice her eyes and ask if she was blind. I always felt a bit mean saying, "Well, she hasn't got any eyes, so…" But people always asked me how she sees, and I had to explain that she doesn't, she just feels her way using her other senses, mainly smell.

It must be exhausting using her sense of smell as her main source of guidance. But Maggie's nose is her most powerful tool. Dogs possess up to 300 million olfactory receptors in their noses, compared to only about six million in ours. And proportionally speaking, the part of their brain that is devoted to analysing smells is 40 times greater than a human. That is why dogs pick up scents that we can't.

A couple of my favourite examples are a sniffer dog in America that alerted police to 35 pounds of marijuana, which was hidden in a container that had then been submerged in petrol inside a gas tank. How you can catch a scent through the stench of petrol is completely beyond me!

And then there's the story of a British woman called Dr Claire Guest, whose dog Daisy alerted her to a lump in her breast that turned out to be cancerous. She credits Daisy with saving her life, because she kept nudging her chest – something she had never done before – which prompted her to check the area. Claire's doctor told her that she was lucky the cancer had been found so early, and as a result of that incident she went on to set up the charity called Medical Detection Dogs in 2008. The charity trains dogs to signal when they sense their diabetic owner is in danger of having a fit, or when someone with Addison's Disease is heading for a crisis.

Scent work is an important way of keeping dogs sharp and mentally healthy, and I do it regularly with the girls at home. I've got a cloth that smells like me, and if you ask Maggie to go and find it, she will. I mean, everything is hidden from Maggie, but she thinks it's a great game and will always manage to sniff it out. I make her sit down in the kitchen and stay there while I hide it, and I can see her bum lifting off from the floor because she's so desperate to get in there and root it out. She knows she always gets a treat at the end, so I think that helps too.

I do the same with Mishka, and she can find my keys for me now. We started off by tying a cloth that smelt like me to my keys, so she had that association in case I ever drop them while I'm out dog walking.

Now I'm working on lavender with Mishka, so I'll put a drop of lavender on the keys and hide them around the house. She doesn't really like the jingly sound of the keys, but she'll still find them.

The only problem is that dogs can sometimes go nose-blind. Nose-blindness is genuinely a thing – it's why police dogs can only work for a certain amount of time before they have to take a break. Otherwise you end up overworking them. A huge portion of a dog's brain is dedicated to smell, so it wears them out really quickly and they can become tired easily. Though I'm pretty sure that's not the only reason why Maggie sleeps so much.

Unless you got up close to Maggie, you wouldn't realise she was blind. For a time I thought it would make things more straightforward if I got her a blind sash to wear – but it just confused people, because they assumed I was blind and she was my assistance dog. So I replaced the sash with a neon yellow bandana that said "blind dog" on it, which was a bit subtler, but still explained why she sometimes walked right into people.

People were really inquisitive about her, and she loved it. The more attention Maggie got, the happier she was. Maggie was clearly becoming a little bit of a superstar in my local area – and my posts about her on my Instagram account were shooting up in popularity too.

I did find myself regurgitating the same stock answers to people who asked about her. It was a bit of a defence mechanism – initially I would break down in tears *every* time I told people Maggie's story, but thankfully I got a bit more resilient over time and managed to hold things together as I told curious strangers what had happened to her. Sometimes I felt a bit heartless, because her story started to roll off the tongue and I'm sure a good few people thought I was being unemotional about it. But that's because I had to teach myself to be. There had to come a time when I wasn't crying about Maggie 10 times a day. It was exhausting, and I'm sure people thought it was a bit odd that this woman they didn't know was sobbing in front of them.

I probably got asked at least five times a day about why she looked like she did, so if I hadn't toughened up a bit I would have ended up sat in my van crying for hours after retelling her tale. That had happened quite enough times already.

From the day Maggie and Mishka first played happily together, I had been seriously toying with the idea of adopting Maggie on a permanent basis. I already knew I adored her, but now that the girls were getting on so much better, it felt like it could potentially become a reality.

I was going back and forth in my head constantly. I kept thinking, "This is crazy, I never meant to get a dog at all, and I've ended up with two in four months!" I tried to weigh up all the pros and cons of keeping Maggie. But I simply couldn't see any cons. In fact, my only worry was whether I'd be able to manage both dogs full-time.

Once I knew that things were solid with the girls and they were really comfortable and happy in each other's company, I officially made the decision to adopt Maggie and become her forever mum. That date was 17 November 2018, and it's one I'll never forget. It was the day that Maggie officially became a part of our family. And I've never looked back.

When I first met Maggie, I had honestly thought that the best she could hope for was a nice quiet life with regular meals and cuddles. I felt she would be fine even if that was all she had. And it would be even better if she could get confident doing a walk along the same route each day, which is what you're supposed to do with blind dogs to avoid confusing them.

I had no idea I was taking on such a powerhouse.

It was impossible not to fall in love with her, and in the end, Mum and I loved her so much that we ended up arguing over whose dog she would be, and I won!

I officially announced Maggie's adoption by posting a photo of her on Instagram alongside a flower and a lightbox bearing the words "I found my home!" I got the most incredible response from people saying how happy they were for Maggie. I also had a lot of comments claiming that they knew Maggie would be spoiled rotten. Of course she would!

As soon as I realised Maggie was staying with me she started to sleep on my bed. Mishka had been sleeping at the bottom of my bed every night since a few months after I first fostered her.

Mishka staking her claim to the foot of my bed had been a gradual process. At first, she slept in her crate, but then she started to come and sit on the bed at intervals, before going off back to her crate. Or she would sit at the foot of the bed and then slope off again when I went to sleep. But before long she was sleeping all night at the foot of my bed. She never came up to cuddle in to me, though.

Maggie decided she deserved the same treatment, and once I'd decided I was keeping her permanently, I couldn't really argue. She just cuddled up next to me one night and I could feel her softly breathing. She was so warm and cuddly, and just the right size to snuggle. It was such a touching moment, and inevitably as soon as I'd let it happen once she decided we'd go to sleep like that every night.

Every evening before we go to sleep I kiss her nose goodnight, and every morning when we wake up I do the same. Sometimes I'll wake up and Maggie will have stolen all the covers.

She doesn't appreciate it if I have to get up in the middle of the night for a wee. She huffs and puffs and makes a strange groaning noise because she's so cross I've woken her from her slumber. In the morning both Maggie and Mishka will have a stretch, and then Mishka will walk up to the bed and say hello to me too. Every now and again Maggie will get jealous and growl at her, which makes me laugh.

Mishka had got so used to my day-care dogs being around that I wasn't sure whether she'd realise Maggie had become a permanent feature of our lives. Maybe she thought Maggie was with us on a rolling day-care contract, and was outraged at the prospect of another dog sleeping in my bed? If she was, she certainly wasn't showing it. I was so proud of how the two of them were getting on.

I soon discovered the one downside to Maggie sleeping up at the top of the bed with me. And that downside is her penchant for destroying my pillows. She starts by padding on them, then she begins chewing them to get them into the most comfortable position for her. She's always seemed to think that's perfectly acceptable, but constantly having to buy new pillows is a dangerous habit. So I let her keep the pillows she ruins, and take care of my own side of the bed. The ones on her side are on their last legs, and are probably covered in slobber.

I know some people don't like the fact that dogs sleep on beds or go on sofas, and it is totally up to people what they want to do, but it's always been a bit of a free-for-all in my house. We're all different with our doggie ways. Some people will happily let their dogs sleep on (or in!) their beds, and some people are horrified at the idea. Personally, I love mine and the girls' night-time routine.

Once Maggie became my second strange bedfellow, I pushed my bed up against the wall because I was worried she might fall out. Every night Mishka settles down at the bottom of the bed on top of the duvet, and Maggie and I both get into the bed and snuggle up. It's like cuddling a warm marshmallow.

If she's still really sleepy, sometimes Maggie will carry on snoozing while I take Mishka out for a morning roam, and by the time we get back she'll be ready for her breakfast. Even if she's still tucked up in bed, as soon as she hears a food packet being opened, her ear pricks up and she decides that there's finally something worth getting out of bed for.

Every dog owner I know has a bedtime routine that's perfect for them. For instance, Eric the Staffie sleeps on the couch, and then he'll go and wake his dad up in the morning and say hello.

Lolli starts snuffling around her mum's bed trying to wake her up, and then she'll put her paw on the bed and wait for permission to climb up.

A lot of people have said to me that they've had to toughen up when they've got a dog. I had very different experiences when I first got Mishka and Maggie. With Mishka, because she was quite fearful and aggressive with other dogs, it was almost isolating at times. Until I got her happier and more confident around dogs and people, I had to be careful where I took her. I also had to get used to being told off every now and again by the dog owners if Mishka was badly behaved. I think that's just part and parcel of being a dog owner. People think when you get a dog you're "just getting a pet." But you're not – you're changing your life.

CHAPTER NINE
FROM PARROTS TO PIGS

When I was around 11, I put up flyers around town and I started walking people's dogs for 25 Cents an hour. I would have done it for free if it meant I got to hang out with other people's animals, but my dad said I needed to put a price on it.

I also fed people's dogs or let them out for a wee if the owners were at work, and I got given an unexpected bonus pet when I was walking home from dog-sitting one day.

An old lady was shovelling her driveway to get rid of the heavy snow, and I offered to help. I wasn't expecting to be paid for it – she just looked like she could do with a hand. We got talking and I told her I loved animals and she replied, "Oh great, I've got a parrot called Buddy that needs a home."

She went inside and came out with this bird in a cage and handed him over to me. Buddy had belonged to her daughter, but she'd moved away, so her mum had adopted him. He was such a chatty little thing that I think she was pleased to see the back of him.

You can imagine my dad's face when I turned up on the doorstep clutching *that*.

Buddy was a winning formula, though, because soon Dad decided that if we had to have a parrot as a pet, he wanted a dog too, to balance things out a bit. So we got a Siberian Husky called Crystal, who came from a local pound. She was about two or three when we got her, and she was a typical husky. In short, she was crazy. She was hyper-energetic and very loud. She hadn't been walked enough by her former owners, so she needed constant stimulation and didn't like being left alone.

As much as he had loved our first dog Zaroff, my dad was not dog-savvy. If he'd thought it through properly, he should have got her into training straight away. I think he hoped she would magically end up being like the brilliantly trained Zaroff, and be perfectly behaved just as she was.

No such luck.

Crystal was an incredible escape artist. She could escape from anywhere, and when you tried to catch her she would stay just out of reach and dodge out of the way. One day she escaped from our garden, and made it out to the front of the house, where she danced around, taunting my brother. My brother was a line-backer for his high school football team, so he used a classic football manoeuvre where he pretended to go right but went left instead. Crystal fell for it, and he managed to grab her. I think she was a bit shell-shocked, and she stopped trying to escape for a while after that.

I was a bit of an awkward teenager, and found it difficult to make friends in school. But Crystal soon became my best friend. When I went out cycling or rollerblading around my local neighbourhood after school, I'd put her harness on and hold onto it and she could pull me along. At that time, we were still living in a small, quiet town in Indiana, so it was very safe.

One of our favourite things to do was go to the nearest pet shop, which was a couple of miles away. While all of the other kids were out playing with their friends, I'd be taking Crystal around the pet store. I'd look at every single thing in there – I loved it so much when they got new stock in – but I never actually bought anything. People must have looked at me and thought, *what a weird child*. But I didn't care. I loved spending time with Crystal, and she loved me.

When I was 14, my brother moved out and my dad and I moved to North Carolina. When I joined my new school, I finally made some human buddies. I felt like I had been so reserved up until then that all my friends had been animals, so it came as a real relief. But it also meant that I didn't have as much time to take Crystal out.

I think she got a little bit bored as a result, so she started scaling the six-foot fence around our garden and going off on all sorts of adventures. We had to pick her up twice from the local grocery store, The Piggly Wiggly, because she stormed the place and jumped up on the meat counter.

Following another of her great escapes, dad and I had to take his truck out to find her. We spotted her, but instead of submitting and coming quietly, she decided she wanted a race. Every time we stopped the truck and got out, she would run further down the pavement. In the end we were driving alongside her, but she kept outrunning us. Eventually she got tired and we stopped the truck and she jumped in – but it takes a lot to wear a husky out and she really showed us.

A year later, when I was 15, my dad got a new job and moved to Saudi Arabia for work, leaving North Carolina behind. It was a sudden change, and I had to leave my new friends behind to move to East Sussex to be with my mum and sister.

I desperately wanted to bring Crystal with me, but sadly we couldn't afford the fees for her papers and transport. So Crystal, who was still my best friend in the world, went to live with another family. I imagine she wasn't happy to be leaving either. Knowing her, she probably tried to skydive out of the hold.

When I landed at Gatwick, the customs officials were really confused as to why a 15-year-old was travelling on her own. I was a nervous teenager with acne and frizzy hair, and I was terrified I was going to get sent back to the US and having nowhere to live.

I think they thought I was either smuggling drugs or I'd been trafficked, so they weren't going to let me in the country. Even though my mum was waiting in the airport arrivals area for me, I had to stay in custody for hours while the officials did a load of checks. One official started firing loads of questions at me. I got all flustered and said, "Erm, what?" in response to one of her questions, and she shouted at me, "You Americans are so rude. You either say excuse me or pardon!"

I am a UK citizen because I was born in the UK, and thankfully I had a load of photos to back my story up. Eventually they let me through and I was reunited with my mum who had brought me a really cute bear to cheer me up, but it was an awful experience.

I soon settled in Steyning with my mum and sister, but it was a little bit of a culture shock at first. My mum kept telling me off for talking to random strangers in the supermarket queue or on the bus – it's just not the British way! There were also lots of language differences to get used to, but I had already moved around a lot, and the US isn't that different from the UK, so it certainly could have been worse.

I missed Crystal very badly, though, so I soon got another little companion – a feisty Chihuahua-Yorkshire Terrier cross called Tootsie.

She was a real character, and she filled a big hole for 15-year-old me. At that point the only two people I knew in the country were my mum and sister, and it took me a while to get to know people at school because they had already formed their cliques. I was so used to my own company that any friends I made were a bonus. I did have some mates, but they were all in random packs and I didn't really have a group of my own, so I was quite lonely for a time.

Tootsie was definitely the smartest dog I'd ever had. I'd got her locally, and my friend had her brother Louis. When I said his name loudly, "Looooouis!" Tootsie would howl along with me. If I said it quietly, she would lower her voice and go, "Oooooooh!"

She could do endless tricks and was easy to train, but she also had a bit of an attitude problem. She once chased a builder down the road barking at him, and the poor guy was terrified.

She used to come and slam her whole shoulder into your leg to get your attention, and then she'd roll around on the floor in front of you so you could rub her belly with your feet. The things dogs do for our love.

School itself wasn't so bad. But because in America we start an academic year behind Britain, I was way behind all my classmates. I had to work very hard to play catch up, and I wasn't allowed to do any of the fun subjects like art. I had to do the basics and nothing else – another reason I felt a bit separated from the other students.

They put me in a curriculum support group to get extra help, but sadly, I still didn't manage to get the grades I needed to in order to stay on at sixth form as I had intended. The sudden move from the USA had been one step too far.

I felt a bit lost and directionless. But not long afterwards I read about an animal school called Brindsbury College in Pulborough – and suddenly I had a ray of hope.

I went through the application process, eventually won a place, and my world changed almost overnight. I had to get the bus there every morning and night and it would often take me over an hour each way, but I loved it so much I didn't care one bit.

Brindsbury was an amazing place. For an animal lover, it was heaven. I got to spend all day, every day surrounded by all kinds of creatures. They had a little farm with pigs and chickens, as well as a reptile house *and* a tropical reptile house. They had a small furries section, which is where the rabbits and ferrets and other little animals lived, and they even had an insect room.

After so many years of feeling like I didn't fit in, now I was truly in my element. Every morning and evening we looked after the animals, with classes in between.

One of our assignments was to train two animals to do something. I was so excited about it I trained three.

The first thing I did was train a pig to sit. I was delighted with myself, but it caused a bit of an issue, because all of the students wore blue lab coats, and every time the

113

pig saw someone in a blue lab coat it would go and sit in front of the gate, meaning they couldn't open it to feed them. When you've got a 200-300lb Kunekune pig rooted to the spot refusing to move, it's difficult to reason with it. So we ended up having to trick them, with one of us running around to the gate opposite and letting themselves in quickly before the pig saw. Pigs are much cleverer than dogs, believe it or not. They're as smart as four-year-olds, and yet we often keep them in tiny crates and don't allow them any freedom.

Some of the teachers used to bring their dogs in, so I trained one of them, a big Doberman, to dance. *Sort* of. I basically taught it to lift its left leg when I said "paw" and its right one when I said "shake", so when it did both of the commands at the same time it looked like it was throwing some shapes.

Finally, I taught some chickens to recognise a star shape. I got an empty egg carton and put a star-shaped piece of plastic in one of the holes. Then I lay a piece of paper over the top and the chickens had to peck through and find the star shape. If they picked the correct hole they got a mealworm. It was like something out of *I'm a Celebrity*. One of the chickens used to sit on my shoulder like a parrot. Chickens are also a lot smarter than people think, too. They can recognise people, they can count, and apparently, they even know how to manipulate each other.

I was one of those students who worked really hard in the classes I liked, and then sometimes wouldn't turn up for the ones that didn't interest me. We had to do a module on running kennels and catteries, and I just thought, *Why bother? I know I don't want to do that in the future.*

There was never another option for me when it came to work. I was always going to do something involving animals. I jumped from wanting to be a farmer to wanting to be a vet. But then I realised that when you're a vet you don't get the chance to forge a relationship with the animals, and that was the most important part for me.

After I ditched the vet idea, I decided I would like to become a conservationist so I could help to save animals. After graduating from Brindsbury College, I got a place at Bristol University to study Integrated Wildlife Conservation. That was where I first learned that in order to save animals, we have to save the world first. We can't just hope for the best. We have to convince people that animals are worth saving, and that means making the world a place they can survive in.

The course was great, but as time went on, I wanted to more time around animals than I was doing. I knew that my future career would involve me being with animals on a daily basis, but I still hadn't worked out my exact path.

Tootsie came to live with me in my student halls, but because we weren't allowed to have pets, every time I went outside past the security guard I had to put her in a bag. I'd say, "Head down," and she would put her little head down. Then I'd say, "Okay," and she'd pop her head back up. She really was a bright little girl.

Sadly, poor Tootsie had a horrible stroke of bad luck. Somehow she ruptured a disc in her spine, and as a result, she lost feeling in her nerves. My mum and I tried everything we could to help her to have a good life, but Tootsie was losing control of her movements. She started to wee herself, and she would get so upset about it. She also suffered from urine burns, and it was horrendous seeing her in that state. In the end, we knew we had no choice but to do the best thing for her. Little Tootsie was put to sleep, because it just wasn't fair to keep her alive in such a sad and painful state.

I didn't stop crying for a week, and even now I really miss her. I miss all of the dogs I've lost.

CHAPTER TEN
WALKIES

I had started an Instagram account for Maggie as a way of sharing the love and positivity she brought to my life, and to show people you don't have to be perfect to be beautiful and loved. In the months following her arrival, it really took off and people started to recognise Maggie when we were out and about. I suppose that she's really quite hard to miss.

It makes me laugh how excited people get when they see her. It's like they've seen a celebrity. They gasp, "Is that Maggie? It has to be, there aren't many blind, one-eared dogs around, are there?!"

She began to get recognised around Brighton quite often, and even when we went to London, we started getting stopped more and more by adoring fans. Everyone who meets her is moved by her, and she's always happy to offer a very wet-nosed kiss, or nuzzle in for a cuddle. She basically makes you love her whether you like it or not.

Another consequence of her Instagram presence was that I started being contacted by people and organisations keen to meet her. In November 2018, for instance, Maggie and I were invited to go along to a class in London called Wildlife Drawing, in aid of the Wild at Heart Foundation. The premise was for artists to draw Maggie in exchange for a donation to the charity.

I took Mishka along too. Mishka had always had her quirks, so I was nervous about how she would deal with the situation. I was worried that she might get scared about being in a confined space with so many strangers and growl, bark, or even bite, so I stayed by her side all day. But the artists didn't interact much or try to approach either of the dogs.

As for Maggie, it was hard to get her to sit still and pose, because she just wanted to sit on everyone's laps. But it was Mishka's first public event, so it was only natural that she was shy and nervous.

Anybody who's ever had a dog with behavioural issues can empathise with how much of a worry it can be. You're always on high alert, thinking they might misbehave at any moment. It doesn't make you love them any less, but it does make you feel more stressed in a public situation like that.

But Maggie is a brilliant reassuring presence around other dogs – they seem happier when they're around her. Mishka was more relaxed than she might have been that day, and I put that down to her being around Maggie. Maggie calmed Mishka down, just as Mishka made Maggie feel safe.

Maggie was generally really good with other dogs, but she could definitely sense when she didn't like one. It was usually the ones that were a bit bolshy and ran up to her with their chests puffed out. She'd pick up on their attitude, and there were times where she'd growl at another dog, as if to say "hey, give me my space."

If a calm dog came up to her, she'd be absolutely fine. She always did the usual customary hellos – she'd sniff their bum, they'd sniff her bum, and then they'd go on their merry way. But if a dog came up and was hassling her and wanted to play when she wasn't in the mood, I would see her lip quiver and she would let out a little warning growl. If I didn't stop her or distract her, she would let out a terrible roar.

She met lovely Eric the Staffie, another one of my day-care dogs – a big dog who has no spatial awareness. He is as fast as a whip, and would often bash into Maggie and swoop her legs from under her, which she did not appreciate at all and took some time to get used to. Eric was difficult for Maggie to deal with because he ran so fast and was so big that he physically couldn't stop himself, so he would end up running into whatever was in his way.

If a big dog ran past Maggie, she'd just stop dead and wait for it to go, and she seemed unfazed by it. But I think she lived in fear of another dog banging into her. She must have felt so helpless being confronted with a boisterous dog she couldn't see. But she showed her resilience as ever, dusted herself off and carried on as normal.

Eric is such a lug. He's so stocky he can't even reach around to scratch his own butt. He's very smart, though, and gets so upset if I tell him off. He once tried to run out of the front door while I was trying to open it and I said, "Eric, no!" and his ears went back as he looked up at me dolefully, as if I'd said the meanest thing in the world. He is so sensitive and still remembers it now – every time we go out he looks at me to make sure it's okay for him go out too. He's adorable, but has some very questionable personal hygiene habits I won't go in to.

So I was quickly getting to know the places where Maggie felt a little more vulnerable, and where she felt safer. There is one park that I started taking her to right from the beginning, and could soon find her away along the path so well that she could wander off on her own quite happily in the knowledge that she was safe. Or if we were in a small group, with just Mishka, Lolli and Lennard, she was quite happy to go off and do her own thing. She was wonderfully relaxed. But if I took her somewhere new, or if there was a big group of dogs that she didn't know, she made her feelings known, sticking with me for security. I soon realised how good a communicator Maggie was.

One thing that really helped build Maggie's confidence was going for walks with new people, without me there at all. Once again, Instagram was the starting point – a guy called Luke messaged me to ask if Maggie wanted to become part of the Dog Walking Society at Sussex University. For months Maggie and I had spent all our time together, but I didn't want her to become too reliant on me, so this sounded like a great way of making sure of that.

The society takes dogs out because the members are mostly students living away from home who miss their own dogs. So they walk dogs for free just for the sheer joy of it, so they can hang out with them.

The first time Maggie went along to the Dog Walking Society, she was a bit intimidated by the prospect of being separated from me among so many other dogs, and she didn't know any of the people there either. I found it really emotional letting her go off without me for the first time ever, because we'd been joined at the hip since she arrived.

I had to explain the commands I used to the students so they could help her navigate her way around, and then I let her fly free. I know it sounds silly, but I was really anxious that something would happen to her, or that she would become distressed if I wasn't there. It's hard being a blind dog all on your own in unfamiliar surroundings. I was constantly checking my phone for updates. But needless to say, an hour later she came back happy and still in one piece (minus the ear she was already missing, obviously).

I couldn't believe how well she'd handled such a potentially disorientating experience. But that's Maggie through and through. People often say to me how incredible she is given the handicaps she has to deal with, and they ask how she's capable of living such a normal life for a dog. I think it's because I've always treated her like a normal dog. Essentially, she is normal. She may look a little different, and sometimes she's a little slower to learn than other dogs, but I have faith that there's nothing she won't learn eventually.

I think people are shocked by Maggie's adaptability, because when we imagine ourselves in her situation, we imagine how sad and hopeless we would feel. But dogs don't wake up each morning and dread the day. They're excited about what's to come, because they live each day as it comes. The world would be a much happier, more positive place if we could all think like Maggie does.

Maggie soon became a regular fixture at the university. Before long she was even walking off the lead, wandering around the campus trying to find people to give her love. If she heard someone she would run straight towards them for a cuddle. She was the society's little mascot in no time at all.

The students loved her so much that they even applied for Maggie to get an honorary degree from the University of Sussex. When I heard, I was over the moon. I don't think they've given out a degree of that type to a dog before, but she does meet their criteria. How cute would that be?

CHAPTER ELEVEN
DOGGIE DAY-CARE

It wasn't until my own third year at Bristol University that I first experienced doggie day-care. By that time I had a new dog called Biaroo, who I named after two demi-gods in Greek mythology. She was a Belgian Malinois crossed with some kind of wolfdog, so she was very over the top and hyper. I got her as a puppy and I absolutely adored her.

Biaroo didn't like being left alone if I had to go to a class, but I couldn't afford to get her looked after. So I made a deal with a lady who ran a local doggie day-care centre that I would work for her for free two days a week, in return for Biaroo's day-care.

I loved working there because I loved being around all the dogs. My work went well at first, but as I began spending more and more time there, I started to see a darker side of the business. Though the woman in charge of the day-care centre disguised it from me at first, it didn't take me long to notice just how often she got angry and shouted at the dogs. The poor creatures were scared of her and terrified of putting a foot out of line. This wasn't the way to care for them at all, and I was furious that adorable dogs like Biaroo could be so mistreated for no reason whatsoever.

It was totally the wrong environment for dogs to be in, and I soon discovered she didn't even have a licence for it. That might not have been a big issue back then, but it certainly would have been if she tried to run the same operation today. Thankfully the government have tightened up the laws regarding dog carers. But in those days, anyone could set up a day-care centre or kennels and not have to register it.

Even though working there was a dreadful experience, I am grateful for it, because it was essentially a crash course in what *not* to do in a doggie day-care centre – and that could only help when I set up my own business later on.

After I graduated from Bristol I moved back to Brighton and enrolled on a business course with The Prince's Trust. I wanted to learn the basics of how to run my own company, something I had no idea about up until then.

After I finished the course I moved up to Paisley in Scotland with Biaroo to try and decide what I was going to do with my life. I had family up there and I wanted a change of scene, so I got a job as a kitchen porter. It was boring as heck, but it was good to take some time out and it helped things become clear in my mind.

While I was there I rescued another wolfdog called Benji, who had been kept in a kennel all of his life and was about to be given to a rescue centre. I fostered him and managed to find him a good home, and that was a real lightbulb moment for me. It felt so good that I knew instantly I wanted to carry on helping dogs in the same way.

Sadly, while I was living in Scotland, Biaroo got ill and passed away. It was a bittersweet time – I missed him like mad, but I also felt that I'd now found a sense of purpose in life that I had lacked before. I decided it was time to go back home and start putting some kind of career plan in place.

So it was in 2016 that I headed back to Brighton with the goal of starting my own day-care centre, as well as helping to foster and rehome more rescue dogs. I posted an advert on Gumtree offering dog walking services, and a lady called Sam called and said she needed someone to start walking her two pooches, Lennard and Lolli.

I drove over to Sam's house, and as soon as I saw Lennard in the front garden I knew I was in the right place. I walked up to the gate and Lolli came running up to me, barking like mad. When a big dog barks at you, your initial reaction is to be fearful, but I could see straight through all her bravado.

Sam walked over and asked, "Do you want to come in?" So I totally ignored Lolli and opened the gate. I think that was Sam's test as to whether or not I would be able to handle her dogs!

In those early days, Lolli and Lennard were my only two "clients", so I had a lot of spare hours, and looking after them just naturally morphed into day-care.

I still walk them to this day, and I love them so much. Lolli didn't fit in with normal day-care criteria because she was good with dogs but fearful of people – hence her reaction to me – so she was the perfect dog to get my teeth into (not literally).

She is ball mad, so I would walk her around local parks and ask random people to throw balls for her so that she became more used to strangers. It also meant that she was interacting with people without having to touch them, so everything was on her terms. She was only fearful, not aggressive, so it worked perfectly – she soon worked out for herself that human strangers weren't so bad.

One day I got talking to a lady called Yvonne who had a gorgeous Staffie called Doris. Yvonne has to go away for work sometimes, so she asked if I did dog boarding. "Why not?" I thought to myself. I already had my boarding licence in place, so Doris became the first boarding dog of my new business, My Dog Day-Care Brighton.

The next dog that joined the fold was a huskie cross called Doug, who lived up the road from Yvonne and Doris and looked really like Maggie. His owner sent him to day-care because he was a real character and he needed to learn to calm down a little bit, so spending a day running around with a pack of other dogs was exactly what he needed.

That ad on Gumtree was the only one I ever posted. After that, every dog that came to me was through was word of mouth. As soon as I started building things up and got more dogs on board, I bought a proper van with crates in the back so the dogs could travel safely and it conformed to all the regulations. I started taking the dogs out into the country instead of parks, and we went on amazing long walks together. I found it easier walking the dogs in the country, because everyone gets to enjoy their space and is pretty relaxed, unlike in the city, where many dog walkers seem pressed for time and space.

The canine world can be a strange one, but I love meeting other dog owners when I'm out and about. There is a common bond between dog owners that means you always end up chatting to people you would never usually meet, and I have met some of my closest friends through my dogs. I'm not as shy anymore, and I'm certain that's because you have no choice but to talk to people when you have dogs. Bit by bit, all the dogs I've looked after over the years have brought me out of my shell.

It's possible to get too comfortable, though. On one of our days out, I got caught short halfway through a long walk with all the dogs. Needless to say, there are no toilets when you're in the middle of the countryside, so I did the natural thing and snuck behind a bush to have a nature wee. I told the six dogs to keep a look out and bark to warn me if anyone was coming. They did a rubbish job. I was mid wee when a really handsome man walked past, saw me, went bright red and wished me a good morning. The *shame*.

Sometimes day-care can be very intense for dogs, to the point where it can be quite damaging if nervous or unsocialised dogs are all left together for long periods of time. So I always had to be on the lookout during my work, especially when introducing new dogs.

It became a bit like doggy dating, because I was able to work out which dogs would get on with each other and which wouldn't. If I thought two would clash, I wouldn't have them on the same day, and I would never look after more than six dogs at a time. It did mean turning down work sometimes, but I wanted my business to be as ethical as possible, and a really fun place for the dogs to come. Whenever I got a new dog I would watch it all day like a hawk to make sure it got on with the other dogs, because they were my responsibility and the buck stopped with me.

For some reason – I never quite knew why – I always seemed to end up with the wonky dogs, or the ones that needed a little extra love and care. A lot of dogs that came to me had behavioural problems and probably wouldn't have fitted into a normal day-care environment because it would have been too much for them. They were just a little bit different and they needed some extra attention.

TOP LEFT: The day Hussein rescued Maggie and took her back to his shelter. **TOP RIGHT:** Maggie's eyes had been shot out, leaving just empty sockets that would weep and caused her immense pain. **ABOVE LEFT:** Hussein did the best he could to help Maggie, giving her a thin blanket to lie on, and chaining her to a box to stop her from wandering and getting lost. **ABOVE RIGHT:** Still pregnant, Maggie was moved from Hussein's shelter to a foster home after Roxanna found her and started fundraising for her care. **BELOW:** Maggie in the foster home. Countless people helped her in Lebanon.

TOP: The very first photo I ever saw of Maggie, taken at her foster mum's house in Lebanon. **LEFT:** Another volunteer with Maggie in the foster home after she left Hussein's. **BELOW LEFT:** The vets took pictures of Maggie ahead of the operation to sew her eyes shut. **BELOW RIGHT:** Maggie's eyes had been left open and weeping for months while she was cared for by different people.

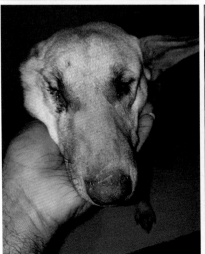

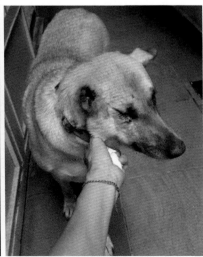

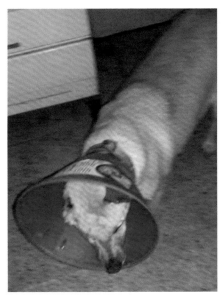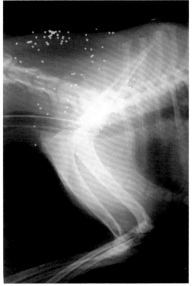

ABOVE LEFT: Maggie recovering from surgery in her Lebanese foster home after her eyes were sewn shut. BELOW: X-rays performed here in the UK show every pellet left in Maggie's little body. ABOVE RIGHT: In the shoulder area there are well over 200 pellets. There are so many that they are impossible to count.

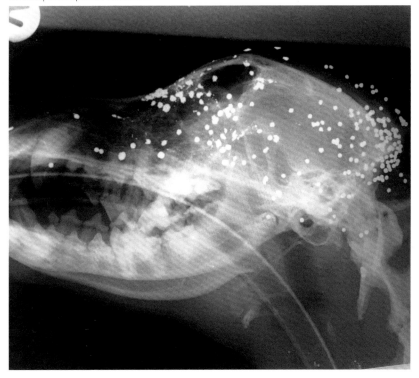

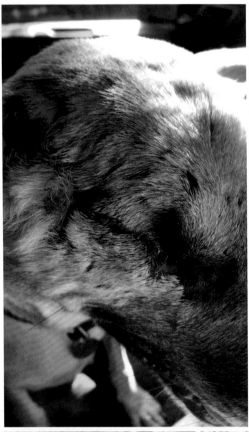

LEFT: Maggie in the front of my car after arriving in the UK. Her scars cover her face and show the pain she once endured. **ABOVE:** A photo taken on our couch that is sweet, but also shows Maggie's traumatic past. She has a wonky jaw after it was broken by her attackers. She's also missing teeth – though she's never had trouble eating! **BELOW LEFT:** Maggie with her best friend Luke, a student at the University of Sussex, where she often visits. **BELOW RIGHT:** While Maggie loves everyone she meets, she does develop some extra-special bonds, and Luke is one of the lucky few.

maggiethewunderdog ✓   ...

View Insights   Promote

♡ ◯ ◁   ⋅ ● ⋅ ⋅   🔖

🐕🐶 Liked by **roxghh** and **61,931 others**

maggiethewunderdog "Dogs are the only creatures that love you more than they love themselves!" @maggiethewunderdog... more

View all 1,113 comments

roxghh The second picture with their massive smiles is

ABOVE: Maggie and Mishka snuggle up together. **ABOVE RIGHT:** The day Maggie passed her therapy dog assessment. **RIGHT:** Maggie and Mishka love each other immensely, though it wasn't all plain sailing at first.

LEFT: Maggie doing what she does best: spreading love and joy to anyone and everyone she can!
BELOW: The beautiful Wunderdog family that we have today: Maggie, Mishka, and the newest member of our family, Millie.

OPPOSITE: Maggie managing her very busy Instagram account.

THIS PAGE: Maggie being Maggie – a very happy and excitable furbaby.

I came up with the idea of doing walking day-care, so I rented a field that had a shelter. The routine was that we would go out for a walk in the morning, and then in the afternoon the dogs could run around freely and just be dogs. Any that didn't want to join in could hang out with me or go in the shelter. It was a really good way for them to learn from each other.

I would play silly games with them and bring along bottles of bubbles or barrels of hay for them to play with. I have lost count of the number of times I've slipped in dog poo or ended up with it on me, and I'm almost immune to it now.

I had learnt to pick up signs in dogs if they were worried or anxious, and was very attuned to it. A lick of the lips or a bit of a side-eye told me everything I needed to know about that dog at that time, and often I'd try to change mine or other dogs' behaviour to make them feel more comfortable, or even give them some time out to relax.

The only dog that came every day was Lolli, because she loves other dogs and she's a natural leader. If one of the dogs was feeling a bit overwhelmed, I would throw a ball and Lolli would chase it, and all the other dogs would run after her, though the nervier dogs would hold back a little.

There were plenty of funny, cute and downright disgusting experiences during those early day-care days. I think Lennard pooing in the back of my van was a low point. We had just finished a walk, so he'd had plenty of opportunity to go. I have no idea why he decided to wait and do it in his crate. Some dogs just have no manners. And let me tell you that what comes out of Lennard does not compare to anything else I've ever seen come out of another dog. Clearing that up was not much fun.

Day-care was hard work, and placed a lot of responsibility on me, but I knew I'd found my calling. I felt more fulfilled than ever before.

CHAPTER TWELVE
CATCHING FLIES

The day Maggie learnt to play fetch was a day I will never forget. I was sat on the sofa at home with Mum, and Maggie was on my lap, with Mishka and Mum's dog Cleo on the floor. I threw a little toy, not thinking anything of it, and Maggie jumped down, grabbed it, and then really quickly leapt back up onto the sofa and kept hold of it so none of the other dogs could get it.

I was gobsmacked. I don't know how she'd found it so quickly. It was sheer instinct. It moved me that she could suddenly behave so much like a normal dog – and at that moment it truly struck me how despite her blindness, despite her missing ear and her wonky jaw, Maggie really was just a normal dog. She must have played like that in the past prior to her injuries, and it was all still there within her.

As soon as I knew she could fetch, I bought her a ball with a bell in so that it would be easier for her to find when we were out walking. For some reason she wasn't particularly keen on it – maybe it wasn't enough of a challenge having a bell inside! Every time I threw it for her, she just ignored it. But every time I threw Mishka's ball, she would barge her out of the way and grab it.

The trick was to bounce the ball so it made a thudding sound on the grass, because that gave Maggie an idea of where it was. I could see her getting really excited when she was following the sound, and then she'd sniff around until she found it. It was the cutest thing to watch. Soon she started developing more devious tactics, following Mishka and then swooping in to grab it at the last minute. We played fetch on our walks together, and I'll never forget the look on another dog walker's face when she saw Maggie run and fetch the ball and bring it back to me. When she realised Maggie was blind, she was speechless.

While she enjoyed a good game of fetch, a game Maggie enjoyed even more was trying to catch flies. It was hilarious to watch. She would hear them buzzing around but she had no way of ever actually knowing where they were. It drove her up the wall, and she would run in circles for hours trying to get one. I was convinced Maggie saw herself as some kind of amazing hunter. When she heard the familiar buzzing sound, her ear would prick up and she'd point her snout determinedly at me as if to say, "Don't worry mum, I'll catch the dinner for tonight" (side note: I do not eat flies). To her credit, she has caught two during the time she's been living with me. It's not a particularly high strike rate, but I still think it's pretty impressive.

Maggie was in so much better shape than when I first got her, and she was a lot firmer to the touch. But that brought its own concerns. I couldn't help noticing more and more that when I stroked her, I could feel tiny lumps and bumps that had probably been hidden by rolls of fat before.

There were three more occasions where I found little red dents in her skin. I still couldn't get my head around what was going on. The marks always seemed to appear on the skinny bits of her – her front legs, her side, the side of her face and her neck. I knew she still had occasional pain, especially around her front legs, and I began to wonder whether the marks were something to do with the injuries she had suffered in the past. A few days after the marks appeared, little round pellets would appear on the floor next to her as if out of nowhere. My first thought was that those little pellets could be tics of some sort, as I was constantly checking her for them. But a darker possibility also crossed my mind – could they be the remnants of bullets, still lodged in her body from her traumatic experience in Lebanon? Whatever it was didn't seem to bother Maggie, but I knew I would need to get to the bottom of it sooner or later.

Maggie's energy and love of life continued to astonish me. She had grown so confident both indoors and outdoors, and she seemed to know herself better than ever. She knew what she liked and what she disliked, and I noticed she wasn't always overjoyed when I mentioned walkies. If it had been raining and it was still wet outside, she wasn't keen on the idea at all. Princess Maggie didn't like getting her paws wet.

She simply hated going out on rainy days – she definitely hadn't got used to our British weather. If we went for a walk when it was raining, she'd sulk, and as soon as we were back home she'd go straight to bed and refuse to talk to me. I always dried her off and put a blanket over her, but she was having none of it.

These moods put me in a tricky situation, though. If I was walking other dogs, she would want to be there, and if I left her home alone she wouldn't be happy with me either. I couldn't win either way. As ever, my approach was generally to take her out with the other dogs, come rain or shine. I didn't want to give her special treatment just because she was fussy about the rain.

Still, Maggie's behaviour on walks had really turned a corner. She no longer jumped up at people to beg for food, she didn't get scared when we were near a busy road, and she could be introduced to other dogs without incident. Of course, there were times when dogs came running up to Maggie and startled her, not realising she couldn't see them. Every now and again Maggie would growl in response, and the other dog owner might tell me to keep her under control. But in instances like those, I felt sure Maggie wasn't to blame. If Maggie was on the lead and it was the other dog who came up to her, it was the other owner's responsibility to keep their dog under control. You couldn't blame Maggie for other dogs taking her by surprise, even if their intentions were good. Besides, most of the time the two dogs are just communicating in a natural way, saying hi to each other or having a play, so as an owner, I had not to worry too much about other dogs bounding up to Maggie to befriend her.

Maggie's social skills had taken a while to consolidate properly, but I'd known from the start that we would get there. Her caring, sociable side really came out when she was playing with my day-care dogs out in the field. When new dogs were introduced to the day-care group and were visibly nervous or shy, it was often Maggie who took them under her wing and looked after them. She didn't have to do that much – her presence just seemed to reassure other dogs, and they were happier when they were around her. Maggie had such a calming influence that I soon began to wonder whether I should look into qualifying her as a therapy dog. She seemed to help other pooches so much that I felt it was her natural calling.

My first experience of dog therapy was back in 2018, before I got Maggie. My mum worked in a care home in Steyning, and she told me that anyone who owned a nice, well-behaved dog was welcome to go and visit the care home to say hello to the patients. I started taking Lennard in, because he was such a buffoon and people always loved him. He was very popular, and I loved the atmosphere of the place.

I knew Maggie would feel right at home there too. Soon after I took her in for fostering, when she was still in the early stages of training, I decided it would be a good idea to take her to the home to consolidate her learning around people, in a calm and peaceful environment. There were no kids running around, and no one was going to bound up and scare her. It was all very relaxed and sedate.

Maggie picks up on the atmosphere in places within minutes, and as soon as we walked through the door back in October 2018, I could tell she felt at ease. It was as if her body language was telling me, "Yes, these are my people."

She seemed chilled out enough, but I could tell she was also really excited because she knew there were lots of humans around, and that meant attention and hugs, which is a cuddle-monster's main requirement in life. As soon as we walked in, all the nurses and care staff came over to say hello, and she clearly thought it was the best thing ever. She was all wiggly and giddy, and once we started meeting the residents she was truly in her element.

At that point we were just visiting for fun – it was only after I formally adopted Maggie that I looked into her becoming an accredited therapy dog. And that was probably a good thing too. I have to say, she was probably the worst therapy dog in the world during that first visit. She quickly got so overexcited that she was jumping up on people's laps and all sorts. A few people had crumbs down their tops, and she really took to those people. If anyone dropped food she was like a hoover, so she also picked up a new bad habit of snuffling around for rogue bits of cake.

Visiting the home would be good for Maggie's training and social skills, and one of my big aims was to get her to a place where she could go and visit the residents without jumping up on them. I knew, however, that would take time and patience.

On our first visit to the home Maggie met a lady called Anne, who was soon to become one of her best friends. We started to visit regularly, and Anne always kept a special pot of biscuits just for Maggie. I had to make sure we saved the treats for the end of the day, so that Maggie didn't think she was just going there for food. It was love first, treats second.

Maggie had a strict routine that she followed on every visit. She would get out of the van, sniff the air, realise where she was, turn around in a circle, and then guide me to the door. She would snake back and forth at the door trying to find the opening, but you have to push the button and wait for them to let you in, and those seconds waiting must have felt like hours to Maggie.

She would then pull me down the hallway before turning left, right and right again, and we would arrive in Anne's room.

Once she'd given Anne a big hug, we would go back around and see all the residents, and she'd finish off with another trip to Anne's for treats. She always fed her way more than Maggie should have been allowed, but I let it slide just on these occasions. They were the *only* times I let her be overindulged, because I knew how happy it made Anne having Maggie there and feeding her. Needless to say, Maggie was over the moon at being showered with treats too!

Anne and Maggie developed a really lovely bond, and have been firm friends since day one. Anne absolutely adored Maggie, and Maggie loved her right back. Every time we left at the end of our visit, Anne would get a bit emotional and say how much she'd miss Maggie until our next visit. Anne's daughter Tracy always sent me cards to say thank you, and she often texted my mum to say how much Maggie brightened up Anne's day. It was lovely to see first-hand how much sunshine my little wonky dog could bring into other people's lives.

I wanted to thank Anne for making our visits so enjoyable and helpful for Maggie's development, so I bought a blonde teddy online, removed its eyes and one ear, and dressed it in a cute little pink outfit to look like Maggie. Anne keeps in on her side table and absolutely loves it. She also has photos of Maggie in a frame and the words "best friends" written next to them. One day we went in to see her and she had secretly done a raffle to raise money for the Wild at Heart Foundation who rescued Maggie. She had raised over £20 from the residents and visitors. Every single penny helps, and I was so touched.

Even though she has no eyes, one ear, a snaggle tooth and a wonky face, everyone who meets Maggie thinks she is so beautiful. And you know what, I'm pretty sure Maggie thinks so too. She radiates goodness, and she's got a bit of a swagger about her. And I love that. She has definitely earned that swagger.

CHAPTER THIRTEEN

MILA

It was back in 2016, shortly after first setting up my day-care business, that I first began working with Wild at Heart. Someone from the foundation saw a post I'd put up on Facebook saying how much I liked working with dogs that don't fit in with the norm, and how keen I was to foster.

They had rescued a little crossbreed puppy called Mila from Bosnia, and she was the sweetest little thing. But she was so petrified of people that they couldn't touch her without her shaking and crying. For a puppy to be like that, she must have had a really bad start in life.

Initially Wild at Heart asked if I could help out by cleaning Mila up. She had been adopted by a couple in Brighton, but they found it hard to cope with her additional needs. She wasn't the dog they were expecting to adopt, and it proved to be too much for them, which

I could understand. She would wee on herself but they couldn't get near her to bathe or wash her, and she found it really hard to adjust to not being on the streets.

Mila needed a certain type of person who understood dogs who had suffered trauma, and her first fosterers just weren't the right fit. I respected them for trying to help Mila, because the poor pup was a difficult and demanding case. At least they had the good sense to hold their hands up, admit defeat and let someone else step in, rather than dumping her at a rescue centre or rehoming her later on down the line.

I have always been happy to take on dogs that can't go to the groomers because they're too scared. I've always been happy to spend all the time they need to get the job done. Even if it takes half a day to clip a dog's claws, I'm willing to take the trouble, and I don't mind it one bit. I don't have all the money in the world, but the one thing I do have is patience, and I also have so much love for animals that I will happily give to them.

When Mila arrived she did smell pretty bad. I had no choice but to give her a bath straight away, and she was so scared about it that she wet herself *in* the bath. It's commonly known that dogs don't love having baths, but it's really not normal for them to be so worked up that they pee in it.

I did everything really slowly and gently, and I didn't touch her head or anything. And I definitely didn't try and blow dry her afterwards. I think she would have had a heart attack. Instead I very gently dried her with a fluffy bath towel.

I gave Mila lots of very gentle strokes and cuddles, and Wild at Heart asked if I could foster her for a while until she became more comfortable around people and could safely be rehomed. I knew I had the right environment for her, so she came to live with me for a little while. I soon realised that while she wasn't great with people, she was brilliant with other dogs.

As with all my other foster dogs, I wanted to give her as much space as possible, but because she was so tiny I had no choice but to pick her up to put her into the van each day to go for walks – and each time she would wee herself again, bless her little heart. She didn't trust me at first, because I don't think she'd ever had anyone who actually cared about her, so how could she possibly have learnt that most people are okay?

She was always walking around with her head down and she used to shake when she was scared. And she was scared a lot. Because she was so nervous, I used to put her on a long lead and then put two collars on her to make sure that there was no way she could run off. Both collars had her ID on them, and then she also had a harness and a connector that linked the harness and the collars. She was like the David Blaine of the dog world.

I took her out everywhere with me to ensure she got lots of exercise, and she began to interact with more humans. Over time, little by little, she became less and less fearful. I would ask total strangers to throw her a bit of kibble, so she began to think of humans as people who did good things for her.

She began to realise that she wasn't in danger, and she also worked out that whenever she got in the van it meant that she was going for a walk. She loved walking so much. When we went out, she always had this look on her face like she was relaxed and at one with nature. Being out in nature is one of the best stress relievers for both people and animals.

I'll never forget one time I took her out for a walk near where I was living. We went past a statue of a man, and Mila thought it was staring at her, so she started growling and barking at it like mad.

I thought it would be good training for her, so I decided to walk her round and round until she overcame her fears and let curiosity get the better of her. Eventually she went up to the statue and took a little sniff. When you see those first signs of a dog changing or overcoming their fears, you feel such pride and delight. There is nothing like it. It's so beautiful when you see them starting to understand that you want to communicate with them and help them.

We came into contact with more and more real people on our walks, and gradually I let them come a little bit closer each time. Eventually Mila even started taking treats out of strangers' hands, which was simply a miracle. She also stopped wetting herself, and that was a clear sign that she was recovering from whatever terrible ordeal she had been through.

Mila stayed with me for about two months until she became more confident, and I decided that if Wild at Heart found it hard to find her a home, I would adopt her myself. But then a lady called Karen spotted her on the Wild at Heart website and fell in love with her.

She drove a long way to come and meet her to see how they got on, and then she came back a second time with her partner, who also loved her.

It was a done deal. After such a bad start in life, Mila had her forever home, where she would be loved, looked after, and kept warm and safe.

Mila is doing so well now. Several years on, she's still quite nervous around people at times, but she's such a happy girl. She's got a lovely brother called Rupert, and they have a great life together. Mila's mum has become a dog trainer since adopting Mila and Rupert – so she's had a whole career change off the back of adopting these two gorgeous little dogs.

People often forget that dogs are complex creatures. There's no such thing as "just a dog". They all have their own personalities and funny little ways, and while certain breeds will have similar traits, no two dogs are ever the same. You can get two boys from the same litter and bring them up in exactly the same way, and one may still be much more confident than the other one, or one may be a terrible food thief, while the other one isn't motivated by treats. Some dogs love to walk for hours on end and cuddle their owners, and others would happily lie around all day on their own sleeping, with little need for human interaction.

Recently I looked after a pair of show Cocker Spaniels, and even though they were exactly the same breed, they could not have been more different personality-wise. They had similar traits in that they were both super needy and really friendly, but they were still individuals and I could easily tell them apart by the way that they acted.

I know someone who has two miniature dachshunds from the same litter. The little girl wants to be on people's laps all the time and needs constant love and reassurance, while her brother does exactly what he wants, when he wants. He'll come over for a cuddle when he fancies one, but it's always on his terms. He is not the kind of dog who needs constant reassurance, but his sister does.

It's not a gendered thing either – sometimes you get very feisty females and passive males, and at other times it's the complete opposite. You could get two males or two females from the same litter, and they would have completely different ways of doing things.

Just like people, dogs are affected by their environment and the way they've been brought up. Like people, they inherit certain traits from their parents, and even young puppies have got thoroughly formed personalities. You can tell from an early age which one is going to be the quiet one, which one is going to be a bit feisty, and which one may be a bit nervous – and there's often one greedy puppy who is right in the centre at feeding time, making sure they're getting their fair share of food. Sometimes you can pick up on the fact that people or animals are shy, and sometimes you can tell from the word go that they're going to try and conquer the world.

And just in the same way, sometimes you choose your pet, and sometimes they choose you. I know stories of people who have gone to pick out a new kitten or a new puppy, and while they've been trying to decide, one of the animals has gone straight over and jumped up at them or licked them as if to say, "You're going to take me home. You're going to be my new mummy or daddy."

So when you get a rescue dog, you have to be ready for it to have its own individual personality, its own moods, and its own past experiences and traumas to deal with. You can't take on a dog lightly, and you have to be ready to undertake some serious training or to deal with behavioural issues.

I wish dog owners had to pass some kind of test where they had to be shown to be loving and responsible, rather than being able to buy pets so easily off the internet. It makes me so angry when I read about people buying sausage dogs to show off on Instagram, and then when they discover that they're demanding little things that need stimulation and lots of training, they pass them off to shelters. That is the epitome of selfishness. You categorically cannot get a dog, whether it's a puppy or a grown-up rescue, and not expect to put in the work. You wouldn't have a child and then not educate it. It's not fair. Dogs are not toys. They are living, breathing, thinking beings.

I read that some people only walk their dogs for 20 minutes a day, and some people don't walk their dogs at all – and that's unforgivable. Do not get a young, active dog unless you can give it a good walk every day. And please do not get a dog if you work full-time and are going to leave it at home alone. Just like us, animals are sociable creatures. Imagine if someone locked you in a kitchen on your own for ten hours a day. You would probably end up chewing the cupboards to bits, too!

On the flip side, as anyone who owns a dog knows, most of us owners develop an enormous emotional attachment to our dogs very quickly. I will do anything to care for my girls, and feel extremely guilty if ever I feel like I'm letting them down. Seeing Maggie and Mishka's little faces when I go out and leave them is one of the toughest things I have to do – the struggle is real! I have such bad dog guilt that I often rush my way through things just so I can back get home to them.

When I get back home, even if I've just popped to the supermarket, from the way they'd react you would think I'd been gone for days. They both go crazy, and I feel so loved. Maggie will paw at me while Mishka stands behind her howling with excitement. It's quite a sight. How can you not smile when you see that?

Even if I've had a terrible day or an annoying drive home, the minute I put my key in my front door and see two waggy tails, I feel relaxed again. Nothing can snap me out of a bad mood like they can.

Sometimes I'll go to into the kitchen for five minutes, and when I walk back into the lounge Maggie will start running around in circles like she hasn't seen me in forever.

If I ever have to go somewhere for work or to help out at Wild at Heart, I will leave the girls with my mum. And no matter what I do or who I meet while I'm out, seeing them again is always the best moment of my day.

I am the kind of crazy dog person that turns my car around just so I can drive past and get a second look at an amazing dog. I have a friend who is equally dog mad – if she sees one in the street, she edges closer and pretends to look at something, and then waits for the dog to acknowledge her so she's got an excuse to say hello. I totally get that, because it's the kind of bonkers thing that I would do. I see people doing it with Maggie all the time. Quite often there will be a bit of side-eye first, and then they'll shuffle closer, and I'll see them look at me as if to say, "Is it okay to stroke your dog?" As soon as I clock somebody doing that, I don't wait for them to ask. I'll just invite them to say hello, knowing Maggie will be chuffed.

Some people prefer the company of animals to the company of people, and I understand that too. I was that person for much of my childhood. The only problem with spending all your time with your dog is that they can develop attachment issues.

Mishka had huge issues with being left alone when I first got her. She hated being on her own when I went out. So when I first took her in, she came everywhere with me so I could make her feel secure and at home. But I knew at some point I would have to ease her into spending time alone.

I started off by leaving her for an hour at a time every day, even if I didn't need to. I used to leave her food in case it was comforting, but because Mishka has never been food-driven, it would still be there, left untouched, when I got home.

So I resorted to simply increasing the time I left her alone, so she got more and more used to me going out, and she also realised I always came back. Trust had been the missing link in her relationships with humans up to that point, and that was the hole that I needed to fill.

Whenever I go out and I leave the girls now, I ply them with puzzles and toys so they've got something to keep them entertained. But Mishka still sits at the window and waits for me, bless her.

CHAPTER FOURTEEN
MAGGIE THE VIP
(VERY IMPORTANT POOCH)

On special occasions, I like dressing my girls up for fun, and in late 2018 my Instagram followers got used to quirky pictures of Maggie and Mishka appearing on their feeds. For their first Halloween together, I dressed them up in some hot dog costumes I bought from Asda, and that Christmas they had matching pyjamas, jumpers and moose costumes. (I got a bit overexcited and went all-out.) Maggie in particular made it known how much she loved dressing up, and her Instagram fans were overjoyed when they saw our silly photos. Maggie was becoming so influential that I had started her own personal account, so she could continue spreading laughter and positivity among people we'd never even met.

I usually look around places like TK Maxx for things to dress Maggie up in, but I never spend more than £10 on an outfit. There has to be a limit when it's only going to be on her for 10 seconds while I take a picture. Maggie now has her own drawer in my cupboard, full of past costumes and silly ideas for future snaps.

I'm always aware of the dangers of the internet and how easily seemingly harmless posts can be misconstrued. For Halloween, I dressed Maggie up as a ghost, cutting eyes out of a sheet and putting it over her head. I nearly put eyes on the costume, but I was worried that people might think that I was mocking Maggie – though of course I would never do that. You just have to find the right way to express things, to show that all the fun you have with your dog is out of love. I've got another light-hearted picture of Maggie wearing sunglasses, which people found really funny because she looked great and they could envisage what she would look like with eyes. It was so normal to me to see her without eyes that I actually found it strange imagining what she might look like with them. But as long as Maggie and her followers were happy, that was all that mattered to me.

Some people would tell me off for posting pictures of Maggie dressed up, saying she looked like she was embarrassed. But being embarrassed is a human emotion, and dogs feel things differently from us. Scientifically speaking, Maggie's expressions aren't actually a demonstration of how she feels – dogs have developed the ability to use facial expressions purely as a way of communicating with us humans. They know that if they look cute and make their eyes big, we're more likely to give them a biscuit! So to say that Maggie "looks embarrassed" doesn't reflect the truth. What's more, I always make sure that my dogs are comfortable with whatever situation I put them in, as I feel that's my responsibility as a dutiful owner.

A dog might not like being dressed up because they don't like the feel of clothes, or for hundreds of other reasons – in the same way that some dogs don't like wearing coats when they go for walks. I know now that Mishka would rather not be dressed up, so I don't take comic pictures of her anymore. Or if I do, I'll make sure she's calm, then pop something on her for two seconds, take a photo, and take it off again.

But Maggie? She has no issue with it whatsoever. I bought Maggie a beautiful yellow sundress from Sainsbury's and took a picture of her wearing it, posing with some Pawsecco, before posting it online. Again, some people claimed that it was promoting drinking, but honestly, it was clearly tongue in cheek and only a bit of fun. Besides, needless to say, there is no alcohol in Pawsecco!

Our first Christmas all together was so cosy. I wrapped up lots of presents for Maggie and Mishka, though Maggie didn't really understand the concept of presents. She kept chewing up the bits of paper Mishka had discarded, not realising that all her presents were waiting for her. In the end, Mishka ended up opening all of Maggie's presents too, but Maggie was quite happy tearing up wrapping paper into tiny little pieces and making as much mess as she could.

I got them both some new balls, and I gave Mishka a giant squeaking snake, which she loved – though Maggie rather strongly disapproved of it. I got Maggie lots of treats, which she was thrilled about, and I also gave them a big blanket each. Maggie had a terrible habit of chewing through any blanket I gave her, but for some reason she didn't do it with furry blankets. So Christmas seemed a good time to get her one, for my own sake as well as hers.

Despite Maggie's hatred of the rain, snow was a big hit from the word go that first winter. Coming from such a hot country, she'd never experienced it before, so when it settled on the South Downs in January 2019 I took both girls up there so they could have a run around. Maggie had no fear about it whatsoever. Once she realised that the wet, cold stuff wasn't going to hurt her, she started eating it. And I'm sorry to report she ate a bit of yellow snow. I'm not going to be the one to tell her.

Speaking of eating habits, 16 February 2019 was a momentous day for Maggie. It was the first time I only had to say "no" to Maggie once when she begged for food. She took herself off to her bed and didn't even try her usual trick of going over to my mum, who is her favourite victim, and whimpering at her instead.

I was so proud of her and how far we'd come. It took her a while to accept that the situation was never going to change no matter how much heart-wrenching whimpering she did, but we got there.

Maggie's social media fame was really beginning to take off, and it wasn't long before her name was in print for the first time. It was in an article called "The top 10 Instagram accounts to follow in Brighton", a tiny little piece in which Maggie had all of three lines. But I was delighted that her radiant influence was spreading far and wide already.

Shortly afterwards, the local newspaper, the *Brighton Argus*, got in touch to say they wanted to do a follow-up piece on her. At the time Maggie had 30,000 followers online, but the piece in the *Brighton Argus* was reprinted by several national newspapers. Her followers started shooting up, and all of a sudden I had a minor celebrity on my hands!

Before I knew it, we had the BBC getting in touch. BBC Radio Sussex and Surrey asked if we would do an interview with them, and my first response was utter bafflement. I wasn't sure how to respond at first – *You do know she can't talk, don't you? She's a dog!* – but then I realised it was me who was going to have to do the talking. I'd never done anything even remotely similar before, but now I was suddenly going to have to be the "face" of Maggie.

My lovely friend Vicky drove me to the BBC studios near Brighton station for the interview, and I was trembling with nerves. Vicky was so supportive, and she waited for me outside while I gave the interview. I didn't know how I was going to keep it together while recounting Maggie's story to a radio audience, and all I kept thinking was "please don't cry, please don't cry, please don't cry." I cried.

I felt it had gone badly because of my inability to put my own emotions to one side – I'd been desperate not to let my feelings get in the way of people hearing Maggie's story. So when I came out, I had a gloomy look on my face and felt like I'd missed my big chance. But Vicky had a massive smile on her face, and she looked me in the eye and said, "You were *so* good!"

Perhaps my emotional style had done some good for Maggie after all, because soon we had a bunch of agents getting in touch wanting to represent us. I felt that the ideal way to tell people about Maggie's story would be for her to appear on TV, so that people could see how energetic and beautiful she still was despite everything that had happened to her. One of the agents I spoke to said he could make that happen for us. I was sceptical at first, but an hour later he phoned me back and told me he had some news.

"Hi Kasey, I spoke to the producers at This Morning. They think Maggie's story is absolutely astonishing, and they'd love to have the two of you on the show."

I mean, This Morning. *This Morning!* When I'd said TV would be a good approach, I didn't expect to land a spot on one of the biggest shows in the country. My mum loved the show, and so I'd been a regular viewer for years too.

"That's amazing!" I exclaimed. "When do they want us on?" After my nerves at the BBC Radio interview, I'd have to give myself some real preparation this time round, to make sure I was absolutely ready to tell the nation what Maggie had endured and how brilliantly she'd pulled through. Hopefully I'd have a good few weeks to steel myself for live TV and to rehearse telling Maggie's story.

"Well," the agent replied, "this is the best bit about it. They've got a slot tomorrow morning! And those slots are hard to come by, so I'd grab it now if I were you."

I was stunned. Live national television tomorrow morning! I was terrified, but desperate to do it for Maggie's sake. And there was also another problem – I had dogs booked in for day care…

I frantically phoned around the owners of all the dogs I was due to be looking after, to ask if there was any way they could find someone else to dog sit for them for the following day. Thankfully, everyone was wonderfully understanding, and shortly afterwards I called the agent back to say we were good to go.

I was convinced Maggie and I were just going to have our fifteen minutes of fame, and then we'd fade back into obscurity. But while our moment in the spotlight lasted, this was an incredible opportunity to raise awareness about Wild at Heart and the plight of dogs like Maggie.

I've always been self-conscious about how I look, so to put myself out there in front of millions of people seemed like a hugely daunting prospect. But I told myself I had to do it for the charity, for Maggie. I had to grit my teeth and get on with it.

I didn't have anything smart to wear, so the day before the show, after dropping the day-care dogs home in the afternoon, I ran into town and bought the first things I saw that looked comfortable and telly-appropriate. I literally ran into a shop, looked at one of the mannequins and bought everything it was wearing. I thought if someone professional had styled that, it must all go together pretty well. Job done!

In spite of the new clothes, I still felt embarrassed about my appearance. I was worried about the fact that this bit of footage would be on the internet forever. I had super short hair at the time, because my mum and I had both shaved our heads for Brave the Shave in aid of the Macmillan Cancer Support charity. We got some of the lovely residents at the care home where Mum works to shave our heads, so we were both completely bald. I had long bleached blonde hair up to that point, and the lady that offered to shave my head was a bit shaky, so it had been a scary experience having her hold a razor to my scalp!

There was literally nothing I could do with my hair to make it look better, because there was no hair to do anything right with. My mum said I should have got a wig, but everything was so last minute that I simply didn't have time.

We travelled up to London on the train the night before, and stayed at a Hilton hotel near the ITV studios in West London. When I say we, I mean me, Maggie and Mishka. How fancy are we, eh? My little street dogs staying at a Hilton hotel. Because I couldn't take the dogs down to the restaurant to eat, I ordered room service for the first time in my life. It was all very new and exciting.

I didn't have much sleep that night. I don't think any of us did. I barely got a wink, and I'm sure the girls picked up on my nervousness, so they were shifting about a lot too. Plus, we were away from home, which must have been confusing.

I'd seen This Morning on TV so many times, so going into the studios was crazy. It was utterly surreal. We got to meet Holly and Phil, who were really, really kind to us, and we had our photo taken with them.

It ended up being a really amazing experience. Holly and Phil both loved Maggie, and made me feel really comfortable. They asked me lots of encouraging questions, and I told Maggie's heartbreaking and heartwarming story as steadily and clearly as I could. Maggie was brilliantly behaved and the response from viewers was wonderful. People were inspired by Maggie and how well she'd coped with all that she'd been through. And I was delighted to have got the opportunity to talk about adopting rescues, and to promote the amazing work of Wild at Heart.

As the interview ended and the show went on an advert break, they gave Maggie a stroke, but they were going straight back live on air after our segment, and I think when they saw how much hair Maggie left behind, they were probably a bit worried about getting their nice outfits covered in dog hair. Maggie shed so much that day I could probably have made a wig for myself out of all the hairballs she left behind on the This Morning rug. If only I'd thought of that before!

Before I knew it, we had another television opportunity, this time with The One Show. I was astonished by how big a platform Maggie was suddenly being offered at every turn, and leapt at the chance once again.

Thankfully, this time I had time to go and do a proper shop with my mum in advance of the show. I bought a new outfit, and also got myself a wig this time. It definitely wasn't the best wig in the world, but it was better than my actual hair, which still hadn't grown out.

The producers of The One Show met us in advance of the show itself to make a VT (video tape), a short film about Maggie to be played during the programme. We agreed to meet them at a dog show on 14 April 2019.

I had entered Maggie into the Best Rescue category for Scruffts, the section of Crufts reserved for crossbreeds. Scruffts promotes responsible dog ownership, and the awards make for a really fun day out that I felt would present Maggie in the perfect light for our appearance on The One Show. Scruffts holds heats at different dog shows around the country, including the one that we went to, All About Dogs, held at Newbury Show Ground in Berkshire.

The One Show came along to All About Dogs to do some behind the scene filming, and you can just imagine how much attention Maggie got. Not only was she wearing her very best bandana, but she was also being followed around by a camera crew! While she didn't win the Best Rescue award, she was still my little champion.

We met lots of people, bought things we didn't really need, and Maggie and Mishka got to hang out on the Insta-pooch stage. One little boy we met was absolutely transfixed by Maggie's one giant bat ear. He kept reaching out and touching it, then looking at her like he was really confused about where the other one was. Needless to say, Maggie didn't mind one bit – she just enjoyed making new friends. I explained to the camera that everyone she meets who shows an interest or gives her some love takes her that little bit further away from her traumatic past.

On the day of the TV show itself, I was nervous but also incredibly excited. The filming in advance of the broadcast had helped put me at ease, and after our appearance on This Morning I felt I knew the ropes a little better than before. I was on The One Show with Adam Hills and Phil Tufnell. I knew who Adam was because I was a regular viewer of The Last Leg. Unfortunately, I had to confess to Phil that I didn't know who he was, because I was living in America back when he was playing cricket for England. Thankfully, of course, he has a great sense of humour and was so nice about it.

The whole episode was about dogs versus cats. Before the show actually started, we did a walk-through of what we were going to talk about, and during that I talked a lot about the Wild at Heart Foundation. But when it came to actually filming the show live, they asked me more about Maggie and Mishka's relationship. Both my girls got a starring role this time, and I was glad to see Mishka enjoying her fair share of attention too.

Phil said that Maggie "makes you feel calm just being around her", and that resonated with me so much. There is just something about Maggie that I can't explain. I do think you have to meet her to get her. She's an effortlessly reassuring presence in a way I've never encountered before. You simply can't define it.

Both Maggie and Mishka were such good girls throughout the filming, and I'm sure Maggie was largely responsible for keeping Mishka so calm amid all the buzz and bright lights.

I wish I was brave enough to watch it back, because I would love to see it, but I still can't bear to see myself on telly. I was worried about being trolled following our TV appearance, so I made a point of not looking at any of the comments online. I knew I didn't look my best, and that's a big reason why I never sat down and rewatched our appearances on This Morning or The One Show.

If someone comes for me, that's one thing, but I knew that I wouldn't be able to stand any nasty comments about my dogs. When Maggie appeared on the website Reddit,

I got a small number of horrible comments from people. Some asked how I could let her live when she looks like she does, and said that she must have a dreadful life. One guy said, "That dog is suffering and she needs to be put down."

Whenever Maggie gets shared outside of our safe community, we do end up receiving insensitive or spiteful comments from people. It can be upsetting, but I had become more resilient as time went on. By now I knew that the best way forward was simply not to read internet comments. Maggie had shown me that kindness is free, and I had no time for hatred in my life.

I only get one bad message out of tens of thousands of positive ones, but they are still difficult to deal with and the best thing to do is to look the other way, and take my lessons in how to treat people from my beautiful Maggie. She, of all creatures, has every right to be angry and negative towards human beings because of what they did to her – and yet she is loving to every single human being she meets.

Attitude is contagious, it really is. Anger and kindness are both contagious, so why not choose the good one? This was the very reason why we started the #bemoremaggie campaign. Maggie makes people happy just by being, and that's not because she goes around handing out cash to people or tells them how good looking they are. She spreads happiness just by being herself. She wants to wrap everyone up in a giant cosy duvet of love.

Some people post comments on Instagram criticising her celebrity status, questioning whether it is fair for her to have so much public exposure. I understand their concerns, because they feel like Maggie is a part of their lives and they have a bit of ownership over her – and honestly, I love that they care about her as much as I do. But to those critics I can truthfully say that everything I do for Maggie has her best interests at heart. As her internet fame took off, there were so many events, endorsements and deals that I turned down because they weren't right for her. Maggie, Mishka and I could be living it up on a Caribbean Island right now if I'd taken everything I was offered just to make money! But Maggie had never been, and never will be, a commodity to me. Her welfare, and that of any other dogs in my care, was and is always my primary concern.

The brilliant thing about Maggie is that she doesn't care what anyone else thinks, so she would never be affected by negative comments if she understood them. She is accepting of herself, and she knows she is wonderful. Humans go around all day worrying about saying the wrong thing, or not being cool or fashionable enough. But Maggie accepts herself exactly as she is, and she doesn't care if she hasn't got the most up-to-date bandana.

She is totally accepting of who she is, which is a wonderful thing, and something I think we can all learn from. She wants everyone to love her, but just as she is. Maggie doesn't think she has to impress anyone or be super cool. She is enough.

CHAPTER FIFTEEN
INSTA—GLAM

Following Maggie's press appearances, her Instagram following just kept growing and growing, to the point where it was quite overwhelming. Her account had gone from being a light-hearted bit of fun, with a few thousand people showing an interest, to having over 300,000 followers – all in just one year.

The Instagram world is made for people like me and dogs like Maggie. I love being creative and coming up with ideas, and Maggie loves getting involved. I'll have one idea for a funny post that will lead me to 10 more ideas, and I have to write them down to remember them all.

The most positive posts are usually the ones that get the most interaction from Maggie's followers. One of my favourites was a post I created of Maggie wearing a bee outfit, saying, "You are beeeeee-autiful." Any time

Maggie's got a little sign up or it looks like she's saying something, people seem to love it.

One of her most popular pictures was Maggie posing with a "free hugs" banner. The idea came to me because that is basically all Maggie wants – and I thought it would make people smile. The kissing booth was another silly idea I came up with. I made a booth out of a cardboard box that my new desk had arrived in that morning. As ever, slapdash posts like that seemed to get the most likes and the most engagement.

Another of the funnest posts I've ever done, and one I got hilarious feedback on, was when I did a spoof dating profile for Maggie. It went like this:

Likes:
- *Long walks*
- *Cuddles*
- *Smelling butts*

Dislikes:
- *Puddles*
- *Flies*
- *Not being doted on and pampered every second of every day*

I think that kind of summed her up. If Maggie were to find her canine match, it would have to be someone sensitive, kind, fun, and willing to share treats and go on adventures.

I took to writing posts from Maggie's point of view on her Twitter and Instagram accounts because it made people laugh, but I also felt like I knew her so well by this time that I could tell what she was thinking. I knew her personality, and I honestly felt like I was channelling her sometimes. She had her own voice in our home and she wasn't afraid to make her opinions known. If social media didn't exist, human Maggie would be on a plinth on Speaker's Corner in London, telling you how the world should be.

I love sharing pictures of rescue dogs, and I guess that's the niche I've found on social media that had made Maggie so popular. That and the fact that we like to make all our posts as positive as possible, to spread the love and raise awareness for the plight of these amazing creatures.

Maggie was getting used to other people taking her photograph, too. She still went to Sussex University on a regular basis to go out with the Dog Walking Society, and the students invited her to presentations and all sorts of other events. When I took her to the Sussex University open day, I got tagged in countless photos on Instagram, where people were posting, "Oh my God, I've just seen a celebrity!" Maggie did her first proper photo shoot at the university, too. Some of the students did some test shots of her, and they were beautiful. I was so proud of Maggie the Model. She could be up on those catwalks with Gigi and Bella, no problem.

It was only a matter of time, then, before Maggie got invited to take part in a professional fashion show – in trendy Chelsea, no less! It was a charity catwalk event called Struts, held by a fancy doggie store in London called Love My Human. All the proceeds of the day went to charity, so it was great to be a part of something else that was giving back.

They had a grooming area backstage, so Maggie had a wash and a blow dry, and she even had a blueberry facial. She had a new lead, collar and bandana, and she'd managed to get her bikini body back, so she was walkway ready.

Some of the other dogs were wearing cool coats or hats, but there were no fancy gowns or designer togs on Maggie. She went *au naturel* and just wore her rescue bandanna, because the show organisers said they didn't want to take away from her natural beauty!

The fashion show was an outside event and the weather wasn't great, so I hadn't expected there to be that many people – but it was packed. I assumed Maggie would just be walking up and down the red carpet just like all the other dogs.

But while we were waiting backstage, Nikki Tibbles from Wild at Heart went out to the front and introduced us. Suddenly it hit me that Maggie was a bit of a big deal now. I often get anxious if I have to walk in front of people or face big crowds, so her grand introduction did initially panic me a little bit. But knowing I had Maggie by my side made me feel so much calmer. Her reassuring presence worked its magic yet again. And her mutt-walk was on point, if I do say myself.

Soon after the fashion show, Maggie had her first professional photo shoot, thanks to a man called Alex, owner of photography business Dogs by Alex. He got in touch via Instagram, asking if he could take some pretty pictures of the dogs free of charge. I was thrilled. It was Maggie's first real modelling experience, and Alex totally fell in love with her.

I wouldn't say it was a roaring success, because Maggie didn't really know what she was doing, so every time we wanted her to look at the camera I had to stand behind Alex and rustle a food bag. Meanwhile, Mishka, who is not usually known for her people skills, took to Alex straight away and was really happy to pose for him. The photos he took were so beautiful that they made my heart hurt.

Ever the fun lover and diva extraordinaire, Maggie now had her own special backpack that I carried her to events in. I put her in it whenever we went on public transport to go to an interview or a shoot, because it was so much easier and safer for her than sitting in a bustling crowd of careless commuters. Especially when we went to London, the buses would be crazily busy, so quite often dogs like her would get pushed out the way. It's hard to notice that Maggie is blind, so I knew that she would be anxious and at risk of injury unless I found a cute solution.

The rucksack is designed so that her little front paws go over my shoulders, and she's at head height so everyone can stroke her. I can feel her little tail going banging against me when she's happy because she's getting love. She also has her own backpack for her poop bags and tennis balls. But I learnt the hard way that I can't leave her treats in there, because she chewed a little hole in the bag and got them out with no trouble at all.

Travelling around with Maggie in a backpack may have looked ridiculous from the off, but I didn't care one bit. It was perfect if I had Mishka with me as well, because I could put Maggie in her backpack, and then focus on keeping Mishka safe on the lead. We had to travel more and more as Maggie's profile grew and grew, and with our comfy, safe solution she was totally fine about going on trains and buses. She might not have loved the journey itself, but it at least meant plenty of attention, and she always knew there was something exciting waiting for her at the other end!

Maggie, of course, was totally oblivious to her growing fame. Not that long ago, she didn't have a home, she had another name, and her future was deeply uncertain. And in just a year, people were stopping me in the street to tell me how much they loved her and what an impact her message had had on them. 2019 truly was a whirlwind. Thankfully, being Maggie, she wouldn't have let fame go to her head even if she had known how much of a big deal she had become.

We met another wonderful photographer, Lucy Reeve, through the Wild at Heart Foundation. She had come up with an idea to get loads of dogs posing as different ABBA songs. Wild at Heart posted online to ask if anyone's dog wanted to get involved, and I couldn't resist. It had Maggie's name all over it. We were straight in there.

We posed for a song called "People Need Love". The shoot was lovely, and Maggie was beginning to get used to the process of sitting still to have some snaps taken. She had always loved dressing up and striking poses, but she had such an inquisitive snout that it had always been a battle to get her to point it in the direction of the camera. But we were managing it better and better each time. Our ABBA photo was of me sitting down with Mishka and Maggie looking up at me adoringly – though thankfully I was mainly cropped out of the final version, so the dogs were quite rightly the centre of attention, as always!

We went to an event held by a charity called Paaw House where Lucy's pictures were on sale, and when I saw someone buy one of her prints of Maggie and Mishka, I felt quite emotional. I couldn't believe somebody would have a picture of my beautiful dogs actually hanging up on their wall. It brought home to me just how much difference these two loving girls could make to the lives of people they'd never even met. And given what they'd both been through in their early lives, it was really special to see them appreciated so much for the amazing creatures they are.

As the Maggie's momentum continued to build, we started meeting several human celebrities too while out on our travels. I'm not much good on the celebrity side of things, and when my friends start gossiping about celeb fall-outs and break-ups I usually have to Google their names to find out who they are. I could walk past a superstar in the street and not have a clue who they are. I see people when I watch TV, but I never remember who anyone is and I am the last person who would know anything about celebrity gossip.

We were invited by Klarna, a shopping app, to take part in a pop-up salon, where you could get your hair and nails done alongside your dog, and they had famous people DJing. The organisers paid for a taxi to collect us, take us up to Soho in London *and* then bring us back home again – I felt so posh! They also pledged to donate a chunk of money to the Wild at Heart Foundation if Maggie made an appearance.

There were lots of Instagram influences there, and we met a guy that I thought was called Marvin Kemp. I was told afterwards that he was actually Martin Kemp. That didn't mean anything to me, and unfortunately neither did Spandau Ballet. It wasn't even much help hearing that his son Romeo was in the Jungle last year. I was oblivious.

The event was fun all the same, and the following day Martin's wife Shirlie messaged me on Instagram to say that Martin had told her all about Mags. She said, "He honestly has not stopped talking about Maggie. He said her energy was so incredible and he felt so much love from her, so if there's anything we can do to help…"

I was touched. Martin had literally met Maggie for 30 seconds, but she must have left a lasting impression.

Oh, and apparently Shirlie is famous too. I wonder where I can find a Dummy's Guide to celebrities?

Maggie was also bagging herself a few famous Instagram followers, including Vicky Pattison, who sent me a funny message one night saying that she was feeling a bit rubbish so she was going to sit on the sofa and eat chocolate – and I said that I hoped pictures of Maggie would cheer her up!

The Instagram world is a fun and crazy one, but I was beginning to feel a lot of pressure to post every day and keep Maggie's followers updated with all her antics. And Maggie's online presence wasn't all plain sailing, either. I was distraught to find that multiple accounts had taken Maggie's photos and were posting them on their own pages or websites. One such account had put a bogus link in their bio for donations "to help rehabilitate Maggie". This was someone who didn't even know Maggie, who was presumably just pocketing any donations that came in.

It made me furious to think that people could take advantage of a dog who had been through such an ordeal and was still giving so much back to the world around her. If these had been fan accounts tagging us in on their posts, I would have been delighted. The more people who see that blind dogs are healthy and can live great lives, the better. But I couldn't believe people would steal her photos and pretend that she was their dog.

You only have so much control over the Internet, but seeing people exploit Maggie like that was hard to take. So I started putting watermarks over certain photos, to stop them being stolen. I knew that there would be certain people who would try and pull at people's heartstrings and cash in. But charities like Wild at Heart work so hard to raise money for dogs in need like Maggie, and it hurt enormously to see people trying to take that cash for themselves.

As a result of the pressure and frustrations of social media, there came a time in 2019 when I decided I needed to take a step back from Instagram for a while. I had been unsure whether to dedicate myself full-time to working on Maggie's Instagram account, or to carry on doing my day-care work. Things had got so busy with Maggie so quickly that I didn't know whether I would be able to sustain both at once. It was a bit of a sink-or-swim moment, and I had to take some time out so I could decide about what would be best for me and the dogs' future.

I had family coming to stay one weekend, so I didn't post anything about Maggie for a couple of days. Within days, I got a lot of messages from people checking in to see if she was okay, and to ask what was going on – and I realised just how much responsibility I had taken on since Maggie shot to fame.

I knew how much people relied on Maggie for inspiration and to make them feel good, and I knew that some people checked Maggie's Instagram every day. I knew that for some Instagram users with mental health problems, Maggie's uplifting daily presence could be a real respite. I certainly didn't want to take Maggie away from her fans completely, and didn't want to let anyone down. But equally, I needed to find some kind of balance, and needed to assess what was in Maggie's best interests.

I knew that some way or other, I would want to carry

on telling people about all the wonderful dogs out in Lebanon that needed homes and were suffering. And if there was any way we could help to fundraise for Wild at Heart or similar causes, we would do that. But Maggie's Instagram account had become so much more than that. It was about bringing real positivity to people's lives on a regular basis. Her goofy, happy face was bringing joy to countless lives.

At the same time, I often saw comments from people crying over Maggie on Instagram, because they were so upset at seeing her injuries. Knowing how happy Maggie was in real life, it hurt to think that I might be causing sadness by sharing Maggie' pictures. Those who know Maggie know how unapologetically awesome she is – she's fiercely independent and has a will of steel. She has more friends that any animal or human I know, and is always on the lookout for more. She doesn't judge and she doesn't discriminate, she just loves. But for people who had never met her, I didn't want to be a cause of upset. Maggie loves to spread joy, and she would have hated it if she'd known people were upset on her behalf. I take on other people's problems very readily, a trait that I am proud of, but I think I had started to feel weighed down by responsibility for people that I didn't know, and I began to worry about how healthy that was.

As a result of that, I decided to take a whole week off of Instagram, just to test the waters and see how it went. It was a test for myself as much as anyone else – I had to try not to feel guilty about not posting as regularly as I had been. I still posted the occasional snap on *My Story*, which had become like a little informal diary of my dogs – I had kept every photo I ever posted – but I needed to have a breather.

This is how I explained things to fans of Maggie the dogfluencer:

As I'm writing this post I can already see the comments. I know many will be annoyed, but I hope that you will also be supportive. We are taking the week off Instagram!

Since starting Instagram I have posted every day, seven days a week. I love Instagram! I have a family on here and incredible friends, and the messages I get melt my heart and fill me with joy each day. Unfortunately I need a break from all the love and joy to focus on my personal life. I am at a crossroads where I need to think about my future and what that holds for me and the girls. I truly adore Instagram and speaking to you all daily, but it is also very time-consuming to run Maggie's account. It's a hobby that in some ways has become a full-time job.

For example, I can easily get 100 DMs a day. If you do DM me then you'll know how hard I try to reply, and please keep messaging me! I love talking with you! I love reading all the comments on each post and meeting new people. As Maggie's following grows I feel so proud and amazed! I honestly can't believe that over 60,000 people are interested in what Maggie does each day! While I'm proud and humbled and I know I'll be letting down quite a few people, it's important for me to take this week off, so I can sort out my finances, personal and family life. I know you'll understand and hope you'll survive the week without us! ❤ *Everyone knows how much I love being a part of this community. It's just that I have commitments I'm neglecting because this Instagram family has become so important to me. As my family and friends I know you'll understand that I need a few days away. I promise we aren't leaving you forever! You will see Maggie's beautiful face again – and Mishka's too, of course!* ❤*

Hope you have an awesome weekend and we will see you at 7:30 UK time, Friday 14 June! ❤

The break was much needed and really helped me settle things in my mind. I realised that realistically, I had to keep the day-care side of things going. That had been my pet project (!) for so long, and I loved all the dogs I worked with and wanted to be there for them. It was also where my basic income came from, and it would have been silly for me to put all my energy into Maggie and Instagram. Ultimately, I love all Maggie's fans, all the comments we get, and it's so lovely when we get sent free food – but I couldn't really pay my rent and bills in dog treats.

I still really wanted to carry on with Instagram, so I found a way to do both things at the same time, by spacing my posts out and cutting myself some slack if I was too busy to post some days. And I found that Maggie and I were all the happier for it.

CHAPTER SIXTEEN

DOG TOOTH

From the day I took her in, Maggie had coped astonishingly well with her physical imperfections. But that's not to say they didn't still cause her any trouble. Her blindness, missing ear, jaw and legs still caused her occasional discomfort, and eventually the day came round when I had to take her to the vet to sort her teeth out and have the two broken ones removed.

The vet's surgery was such a sad place to be. It was full of pet owners who were stricken with worry or grief over their beloved animals. There were so many tears in the waiting room that I felt very wobbly about Maggie after I dropped her off. For the vets themselves, it must be so hard working there and having to see animals in pain on a daily basis. All they want to do is make them better, and yet they have to deal with this throughout their working lives. The agony and suffering that some animals have to go through must be horrendous, and they have to do their best to patch them up.

I couldn't imagine for a second what it must be like for them to have to tell people that they're going to lose their pets. I couldn't believe how brave you had to be to try to save an animal and then be responsible for telling its owner if it isn't possible. It seemed incomprehensible to me that I had ever considered becoming a vet.

Thankfully, Maggie's operation wasn't as serious as all that, but all the same I hated being without her that day. I was upset at the thought of her having to wait in a crate for hours on her own. She must have been able to hear people walking past her all day, and I could just imagine her little tail wagging because she wanted love from them. Because she couldn't see, she wouldn't have known where she was and what was going on, and she wouldn't understand why all of these people weren't stopping to cuddle her.

Thankfully, my teenage little sister had a friend who was doing work experience at the vet's that day, so she kept sending photos of Maggie to my sister to let her know that she was okay, which helped to keep me calm.

The vet knew about Maggie's lumps and bumps from my previous visits, and he had kindly offered to take some X-rays of her body while he she was under sedation. I gratefully accepted, hoping that this would finally be an opportunity to better understand the true cause of some of her physical peculiarities.

I called the vet in the afternoon to check up on Maggie, and they said that they would give me an update in an hour, so I took the opportunity to go out for some fresh air with the other dogs. I left my phone charging at home, because I wasn't expecting the call for another hour, but when I got back I had two missed calls and two voicemails.

My heart missed a beat. Because they'd called sooner than expected, I was anxious something had gone wrong, and initially I was simply too scared to listen to the messages in case it was bad news.

Thankfully, though, Maggie was absolutely fine. The messages were just telling me that I could go and pick her up, and my relief was unbelievable.

After seeing so many tears at the vet's that morning, I had brought some doughnuts to cheer up the poor people in the waiting room. And when I arrived, Maggie was getting a lot of fuss and attention – normal service had resumed! Even though she'd just an operation on her jaw, Maggie had still managed to shovel down some food, which made me smile. Even if Mags didn't have any teeth at all, she would still find a way to eat.

She was quite drowsy and a bit all over the place, but Maggie was so happy to see me. She was making these funny grunting noises, and if I didn't know any better I would have sworn she was drunk. I had brought her favourite blanket with me – a massive grey furry one that's full of holes where she's chewed it up. I knew it would comfort her.

I went to see the vet for Maggie's X-rays. The operation had been a success, but he had a concerned look about him when I entered the room.

"Kasey," he began, "you were right about these lumps under Maggie's skin. They're bullets from where she was shot. Those pellets you keep finding on the floor are fragments of bullet that are working their way out of her body."

I was shocked, though it shouldn't really have been a surprise. "When I first got her," I said tentatively, "Maggie's rescuers said they thought she'd been shot 17 times. But I've already seen five pellets come out of her. Did you find more a lot more pellets in her, or are there fewer than we thought?"

The vet shook his head. "More. Many more."

"How many? 20?"

"Kasey, there's no way of saying this kindly, but there are so many fragments of bullets and shrapnel in Maggie's body that it's physically impossible to count them all."

I was stunned. How could Maggie be such a positive and fun-loving dog, and yet her injuries were so, so much worse than I'd ever imagined? I stared at the vet in dumbfounded silence, and he turned to pick up the X-rays.

When he showed me the scans, I couldn't even speak. I am an emotional person – I cry at literally anything – but those images were too much. I had no words.

The bullets were *everywhere*. Literally, her whole head and body was littered with them.

A lot of the ones that showed up on the X-ray were bird shot, so they were absolutely tiny, but I counted the specks of metal in her shoulder area and there were 74 there alone. It was awful to witness. But I took some small comfort from the fact that at least I now knew a little better what we were dealing with.

The vet was right – it would be impossible to count them all. The only way we would have been truly able to assess it was by having a CT scan, but that would have cost a lot of money and it didn't seem worth it. I didn't want to put Mags through more trauma than absolutely necessary.

The pellets lodged deeper within Maggie were bigger, so the vet's conclusions were that Maggie had been shot three or four times at close range with a shotgun, and then with a BB gun from further away. I already knew that Maggie had survived some horrendous experiences, but it was all too much to take in.

The fact that Maggie had suffered even more than anyone could have imagined was beyond comprehension. Even the vet, who was usually really happy and upbeat, seemed sombre.

But thankfully, the X-ray gave us cause for a chuckle too. We couldn't help laughing when we both saw how small her brain was. Maggie has a brain the size of a walnut, which I must admit wasn't a massive surprise to me. Even though she picks up commands very well, I don't think she's the sharpest pencil in the box. She can be so daft when she wants to be.

The vet advised me not to try to take any pellets from Maggie's body. He said they would come out in their own time, as I had already seen them do. After seeing the X-rays I knew for sure that those little metallic pellets were bits of shot that had made their way out when they were ready. They were still the same shape they were when they left the gun and entered her.

The kindest thing to do for Maggie was to leave the pellets in for now. There were so many that it would be unbearably painful to go in and try to remove them all. It would involve multiple surgeries and take endless hours.

A small number of the shots had become fragmented into tiny pieces, so they would be especially hard to remove. If anything got infected or there was an obvious way that it was affecting Maggie on a day-to-day basis and we knew that we can take the pellets out and not cause her any additional pain, I would absolutely agree to it. But when I'd asked vets about her physical condition before, they had always assured me they didn't think she was in any pain – and that was the most important thing for me.

The vet suggested that medication could be a helpful option for Maggie, but I wanted to wait and see how things went first, because I didn't want her to have to be on certain drugs for the rest of her life. But I certainly wasn't firmly against the idea. On a day-to-day basis, though, she had always been fine in the past, and the bullets had never seemed to affect her much. As long as that continued, I was happy to keep going as we were. The vet agreed with me, and I took my lead from him, because he knew best.

Maggie seemed chirpy enough after her surgery, but soon as we got into the van, she withdrew into herself and seemed suddenly grumpy with me. Her jaw must have been very sore from the dental work. As soon as we were alone together, it was like a switch had flipped and she'd suddenly snapped, "That's it, mum, I'm not talking to you." She seemed genuinely cross that I had just put her through such an ordeal. She definitely wasn't her usual sprightly self, but I was only doing what was best for her.

Ordinarily Maggie wants love all the time, but that evening she just wanted to be on her own. Most nights when I'm on the sofa she will bowl up and bang her head right into me and shove it under my arm so that I have to give her a cuddle, but there was none of that that night. I think she was scared I might hurt her sore jaw if I hugged her.

That night she was clearly in pain and kept making hopeless, heartbreaking whining noises. Hearing that made me wonder if they were the same noises she made when she was suffering and so alone in Lebanon, and the thought was devastating. She usually sleeps in my bed, and we usually spoon – she's the little spoon and I'm the big spoon, cuddling her – but she must have been hurting a lot that night, because when I went to hug her she got out of the bed and went and slept on the sofa all night instead.

When we went for a walk the following day, Maggie went to get in the van. She usually used her whiskers to find out where the door was before jumping up. But I think she must have still been a little bit disorientated, and she bumped her nose on the side of the van and yelped. I felt like the worst dog mother in the world.

Because her mouth was so sore, I had to feed her wet food for a few days. But even though she was getting all these really fancy expensive dinners, it still took me a little while to win her over again. I suddenly realised how much I'd spoiled her since I took her in. You would never have known she was a street dog by the way she acted nowadays. I'd created a monster!

I kept a close eye on Maggie in the weeks after her op and my discovery of just how badly she had been injured in Lebanon. I did all I could to make things comfortable for her and to work out what the best plan of action was going forward. At a pet shop near home, I got talking about Maggie to a woman who told me a similar story about a lasting injury. Her sister had fallen through a blast patio door and had uncountable little shards of glass stuck in her, and two years later she was still pulling pieces of glass out from the inside of her mouth. Her body recognised it as a foreign object and tried to reject it. Likewise, Maggie's body found a way of just working the bullets out.

I felt I was doing the right thing by leaving Maggie to it, but I was still concerned about the pellets still lodged in her eye sockets. They must have been horribly uncomfortable. Imagine how irritating it is if you get a bit of grit in your eye. Maggie must have had to deal with that feeling, only hugely magnified, all day, every day. I just pray she got some respite from her pain when she managed to sleep. She still had all the muscles in her eyes, so when she heard something she still looked in its direction instinctively. That meant that even though her eyes had been shot out, she would still have been moving them all the time. It must have been horrific, and so frustrating.

She wasn't born blind, so she knows what the world looks like and I am grateful for that, but sometimes I wondered if that would cause her more suffering, having the beauty of the world torn away from her so cruelly. I can't imagine what it must be like not being able to look at a tree and see its beauty, or to eat a meal without appreciating how it looks.

The vet had informed me that Maggie had also retained some nerve damage from her ordeal in Lebanon, which explained the occasional tremors in her neck. I spoke to a friend who has fibromyalgia, who described one of her symptoms as being like electric shocks jolting down her face. I wondered if Maggie suffered from a similar thing. But she was still proving herself to be a tough girl. She had never been aggressive towards vets, even when they were touching parts of her that were sensitive or damaged. She had been through so much that perhaps she was resigned to enduring pain, or she was simply desensitised. Either way, she was probably putting up with a lot more than I could have, and I adored and respected her all the more for it.

As well as having her teeth removed, Maggie had to go to the vet with an ear infection on two occasions in the time I'd had her. Her big ear was fine because air can flow in and out easily, but her no-ear ear (you know what I mean) was a persistent problem. Because of the extensive damage, she had a narrow ear canal on that side. The cartilage that held the canal in shape was misshapen, much like cauliflower ear in rugby players. Because it had been sewn up and the cartilage had bubbled, whatever got in there became trapped.

You can always tell when a dog has an ear infection because it tilts its head to the side. I knew there was an issue when Maggie started tilting her head to the left-hand side, and I could see the muscles twitching underneath where her ear should be. The first time it happened was soon after she tripped and fell into a river. I didn't think about it at the time, but afterwards I realised she must have got some dirty water or bacteria trapped underneath the cartilage, which then caused an infection.

The second time it happened was when she went to the groomers, and she got water trapped underneath her ear. About three days later she started scratching the area, and I could tell that it was really sensitive. Both times she had to have antibiotics, and thankfully the infections cleared up really quickly. I learned to take cotton buds with me whenever she went to the groomers, and to clean out the area straight afterwards to make sure that nothing was trapped and there was no water underneath.

The groomers were like a form of torture for Maggie. She always tried to hop out of the tub when they bathed her, even though they kept the treats flowing. When Maggie isn't persuaded by food, you know she's unhappy. I always felt like a terrible person when I dropped her off for de-shedding. There was only so much I could do, and sometimes Maggie's coat needed a professional touch!

Besides, both of my girls had terrible habits of rolling in the most disgusting things they could find when we were out on walks. But I only took them to the groomers when things got really desperate. If Maggie did roll in something terrible, I'd just wash her with doggie shampoo and give her a good rinse, and that did the job fine. At the end of the day, she's a dog – she's never going to smell like Chanel No 5.

Even though her ears were an issue, as a friend pointed out to me, Maggie at least didn't have to worry about getting soap in her eyes when she went to the groomers. Every cloud…

The worst thing about dogs being ill is that you can't explain to them what's going on. They don't understand why you're giving them horrible tablets to take, and they don't know it's just because you care and so you can make them feel better. Maggie had always been such a greedy dog, but getting her to swallow a pill was one of the hardest things in the world. The medicine decoy soon became my best friend.

I came up with a trick where I put a tablet in a piece of cheese and then covered it with peanut butter. That way Maggie couldn't smell the tablet – all she could smell was the delicious food. Then to make sure she didn't get a whiff of the tablet while she was eating the cheese and peanut butter, I'd hold another little piece of cheese against her nose so that all she was getting was the wonderful whiff of cheese.

It might not have been the best thing for her weight, but it did the job and helped get her better. And as long as I could keep the smile on Maggie's lovely, goofy face, I knew I was doing something right.

CHAPTER SEVENTEEN
THERAPY DOG

I signed both Maggie and Mishka up to the Kennel Club's Good Citizenship scheme, a rigorous training programme that is also a really good socialisation opportunity for dogs, and different to anything they've done before. Any dog that's completed any level of the obedience training can take part in the scheme, and in my opinion it's the best course you can do. A lot of trainers will teach using their own methods, but the Kennel Club's training is officially recognised, and it's so stringent that unless you get everything completely right you don't pass.

The idea is essentially that you get a bunch of dogs together and pay £60 for 10-week course, and once all the dogs are ready, they can all go for their award at the same time. There are usually around six to ten dogs in a class – all the dogs are doing it together, like they're in a team. It's a lot of fun and very cute to watch, as well as being excellent for the dogs and their owners.

My reasoning for entering Maggie was that, believe it or not, one day I want to enter Maggie into Crufts. That's my ultimate goal. I want to see my little wonky disabled rescue dog in the show ring with all these fancy hoity-toity breeds, to show that she's just as good as them.

Maggie got her bronze award for the Good Citizenship scheme, and she's now working towards silver. There are some training activities that are harder for Maggie because she is blind, but sometimes it's actually an advantage. One of the hardest bits of the test for the silver and gold awards for a lot of dogs is that they have to sit and wait in a "down" position for two minutes while their owner is out of sight. They can't get up – they have to stay completely still. And guess what? Maggie does it brilliantly, because she doesn't always realise when I've snuck away. She can probably still smell me, so she thinks I'm there – which makes that part of the test a whole lot easier.

True, sometimes she can just sense I've left the room, and if any of the other dogs start moving around she wants to start moving around as well, but we are taking it step by step and she's doing really well. Considering we have to do everything by sound rather than sight, she is doing an extraordinary job.

I practise the staying exercise at home with Maggie and we've built up to a whole minute, so we're doing well, and I don't think it will be long before she'll be able to do the full two minutes.

The trickiest thing is teaching Maggie to walk to heel. As a blind dog, it's really hard for her because she can't see where I am or pick up on hand commands. She can hear me tapping my leg, but she doesn't know where my leg is.

She's used to being out in front in the lead, taking commands from me – and suddenly I'm asking her to walk right next to me, which is disorientating for her. There have been a couple of times where she's got under my feet and almost tripped over, and she's not too happy when that happens.

Sometimes we'll walk along with Maggie resting her chin in my hand, and we are a bit slower than everyone else, but she does it patiently and obediently, bless her. The whole idea is to get your dog to touch your hand with their nose every time you tell them to. But of course Maggie can't see my hand, so I've started putting liver paste on my palm and cupping it over her nose. She's such a glutton she'll walk beside me with her nose pressed against my hand, sniffing away.

People and dogs are so much more alike than we realise. So many people were in uproar when a programme called How to Train Your Baby Like a Dog aired on TV, but there are actually many ways in which human and dog training are similar.

All training is based on Pavlov's dog theory. It's effectively a four-square grid of positive enforcement, negative enforcement, positive punishment, and negative punishment. You introduce something and you can take it away – it's that simple.

Whenever you're potty training a baby, you reward them when they wee in the right place, and it's the same with dogs. If they wee outside rather than in the house you'll tell them how good they are and maybe give them a treat, which is positive reinforcement.

Mishka has already done the first few steps of her training, and as soon as Maggie has got her silver and gold awards, Mish will be going for her bronze, silver and gold too. I did try taking them both along at the same time, and I also tried taking them on alternate weeks, but it just didn't work out time-wise because they were both getting behind. It's much better to do the course with one of them at a time. Because Mishka had already done an extensive amount of training with me, I thought Maggie would benefit more when we first signed up.

I know some people might think it's strange that I go and do a training course with my dogs when I'm a dog trainer myself – but when I'm doing day-care I'm always the one in charge, so actually it's lovely to be able to step back and not be in the position of responsibility. It also gives me an opportunity to learn and hone my own practice.

Often I'm working all day training other dogs, and I don't then want to go home and spend the evening training my own dogs. Doing the Kennel Club course means that I can focus their training and contain it to that one hour each week. It's also a time for me and my dogs to be together and strengthen our relationship.

I can teach them a lot, but there's nothing like being in a trainee environment, and it gives me a whole hour a week where I'm totally dedicated to training them. Plus, I can share resources and ideas with all the other dog owners, and it's a great way to get Maggie and Mishka to integrate with dogs of all shapes and sizes. I also think that it's great when you can teach your dog tricks, but teaching them manners is far more important. It's a lifelong set of tools you can use every day.

My other big project with Maggie was to get her registered as an all-round therapy dog. This turned out to be a bit of a struggle, due to the complications caused by her blindness. But in terms of behaviour, Maggie proved exemplary.

To become a qualified therapy dog, you have to do a one-off test where your dog ticks all the right boxes. The dog can't be fearful of noise – and I'd laboriously trained that out of Maggie in the early days. They must be fine with being pulled around and cuddled – Maggie couldn't be happier to oblige. They can't be afraid of things like wheelchairs or mobility scooters, and they have to be really good with loud noises – again, nothing could bother my Maggie now.

They're also not allowed to jump up when there is food around. Needless to say, I was nervous about that part of the test. But by some miracle, Maggie held her nerve and kept her self-restraint even when all her gluttonous instincts must have been urging her to do the opposite. The fact that this hungry street dog of old could now wait patiently, trusting that humans, who had once treated her so cruelly, would be there to give her her next meal, brought a tear to my eye.

Maggie had become a really calm, confident dog, which is why I knew she would work so well as a therapy dog. It's fun when dogs are excitable, but sometimes older people's skin can tear and bruise very easily, so the last thing you want is a bouncy dog leaping about in a care home, jumping up at people and licking them.

Another issue with her registration, though, was the fact I fed her on raw food. Because of the bacteria in raw food, you can't take dogs who live on a raw food diet into hospitals or hospices, or anywhere where there are people with weakened immune systems. We had been invited to go and visit the burns unit at a hospital, which I was desperate to do, as I thought Maggie would be such a comfort to the patients. I thought some of them might be able to identify with Maggie, and would hopefully feel uplifted by her visit. So I decided to change Maggie's diet to a pre-cooked one, to eliminate the bacteria risk and allow us to make the visit and undertake similar ones in future.

Many of the therapy events that I started going to with Maggie came about simply because people messaged me on social media to invite us. Maggie's reputation was beginning to precede her, and carers or schools were often keen to have her for the day to inspire and comfort the people in their charge.

The first visit we made once Maggie had officially passed her therapy dog exam on 30 June 2019 was to go into a primary School in East London to do a talk about bullying. Because Maggie's got such a sad story, we wanted to show the kids that you can overcome bullying and bad things that happen to you, and come out the other side happier than ever. We told them how Maggie was physically affected by what happened to her, but also how words can be just as harmful.

I was worried the kids might think Maggie looked a bit sad, so I got some of her toys out and we played a lot, because I wanted to show them how happy and active she is. I didn't want any of them to go away feeling sad about what happened to Maggie. When I told her story I told a very diluted version, because I didn't want it to be traumatic for the younger children. But I could still barely get through the presentation without crying. I had to bottle things up to keep it together.

I asked the kids what they thought about when they saw her. I assumed they would all say things like "she's got a lot of scars" or "she's blind" – but, to my astonishment and delight, they all said she was beautiful and seemed happy. You will not be surprised to hear I cried my eyes out at those lovely comments. It was so amazing that they could look past her injuries and see the real her.

We had a drawing competition and all the kids drew pictures of her and wrote sweet things about her. One of them said "nothing can bring you down", and another one said "you're so strong not even a bullet can stop you".

Another girl drew a gorgeous picture and spelt out Maggie's name and put words next to each letter, so it looked like this:

M = Marvellous
A = Amazing
G = Great
G = Gorgeous
I = Intelligent
E = Eager

We also had a giant cardboard cut-out ear, and all the kids got to write things that they want to say to Maggie on there. Whether it was sending messages of love or words of encouragement, they could write whatever they felt.

Again, we got the cutest comments. They all got to come up and give her a little stroke and told her what they'd written about her on the ear, and I was in bits.

It was a truly wonderful experience, and I hoped that in the future we could go into some more schools and continue to spread the word in the fight against bullying.

We also got invited along to Eastbourne Police station's open day as part of mental health awareness week, and that was really quite something. All we did was walk around saying hello and chatting to people, but Maggie was a real hit. There were lots of good-looking policemen there too, and I was trying to encourage Maggie to sidle up to them!

I was talking to a couple of people from the police forensic team, and they told me they hadn't slept the night before because they'd been on a call out. They said that Maggie was the best tonic they could possibly have had, and that she'd really made their day. I mean, you can't get better than that, can you? Who wouldn't love it if they were stressed out and a cuddly one-eared dog showed up to snuggle with them and give them some love?

When it comes to therapy work, it is brilliant that Maggie is so sociable – she will never, *ever* get bored of being cuddled and given love. But even so, I always take her out for a walk before we go to an event or to her therapy visit, just so she can release some of her energy. Because she loves people so much, I need to be sure she won't too hyped up when we get there, especially if we're visiting a hospital or an old people's home. That way, when we arrive somewhere, she's already nice and relaxed.

Sadly, we can't do everything, because we still have to go about our daily lives and I have other dogs to care for, but I do as much as possible, and both of us absolutely love it. And if Mishka can join us too, it's a huge bonus, because we all love hanging out together.

In America, they have a programme where dogs in kill shelters (a heartbreaking type of shelter where dogs not rescued after a certain length of time are put down) are taken into prisons. The prisoners train and look after the dogs, and then at the end of the course the dogs get a home and the prisoners get qualifications. A similar programme is being run in Scotland, and I would love to help do something around where I live.

People are just the same as dogs. They are products of their environments and how they are raised. Everyone is capable of change. The idea of dogs helping to turn someone's life around fills me with hope. I sincerely hope that Maggie can help bring new life to people in the same way.

CHAPTER EIGHTEEN
LOVE IS BLIND

Apart from when I lived in Scotland after my studies, until 2019 I had been living with my mum ever since I first moved to the UK almost 10 years previously. But I had known for a while that it was time for me to get my own place for me and the girls.

I wanted to stay around Brighton where I was already living, but I had to wait until I could get some bits and pieces together. I only had what was in my bedroom, and some plates and bowls that my had mum bought me. I didn't own any furniture, but luckily the place I found came partly furnished.

Living in Scotland had already given me a taste of what it was like to live alone, so I wasn't worried about how I would adapt to a new house, but I was worried about how Maggie would adapt. I took her to the house a few days before we moved in so that she could become acclimatised to the place. Because the furniture was already in place, it gave her a chance to have a really good sniff about and get used to it before I moved any of my own stuff in. That way she would have an idea of the layout and would hopefully feel more comfortable with the move.

There was a lot of coming of going during the first few days after I moved in. I had to do some decorating and I didn't want to end up with a multi-coloured Maggie, so she and Mishka stayed with their grandma as I moved all of my stuff out. But as soon as the decorating was done, we were all set to move into our new place.

The new place was out in the country, so there were a few new things for Maggie to get her head round. There were horses roaming freely around the field that backed on to our house, and I could tell straight away that Maggie wasn't keen. She may not have been able to see them, but perhaps it was their smell that she found off-putting. She certainly didn't like the sound of horses' hooves clopping along the pavement if we encountered a rider in the street, but that was just a peril of living in the country that she would have to get used to. She was fine with cows and sheep, as long as they were behind a fence so that the animals felt safe and Maggie felt safe.

Living in the countryside was also a lovely excuse to go for even more scenic walks. People find it funny that I take Maggie to places that have nice views, but I swear she gets it. She seems to have more of a spring in her step when we go somewhere pretty. I'm sure can "see" what's around her in some small way. She smells space and she feels the wind and sun on her face. I'm certain she senses when we're somewhere lovely. After we moved, I became even more convinced that Maggie could smell a good view.

The dogs settled in remarkably quickly. The house soon felt like home, and the girls loved the fact that there was a pet shop, Gatleys, a stone's throw away. The first time I ever took Maggie there I put some toys, a new collar and a few other bits in my basket. I realised I'd forgotten dog treats, so I ran back to the pick 'n' mix section, and when I got back to the till another shopper had paid for all of my shopping because she thought Maggie was so wonderful. She had already left, so I couldn't even thank her, but it was such a beautiful moment. I stood at the till in tears.

Miss Maggie could be such a diva at times. We could see Gatleys from my house, and when Maggie went outside to do her business she occasionally tried to sneak off there. As we were out in the country now, all she had to do was cross a field to get there. She could smell her way, and it had automatic doors so she could just let herself in. The first time it happened, I caught up with her seconds too late to stop her snuffling around the treat aisle!

If I could sense she was about to try and do a runner, I'd call her, and she'd turn around and "look" at me, but then just carry on out. Sometimes I could lure her back by shaking the treat jar, but if she was really in the mood to go "shopping", there wasn't much I could do to stop her apart from actually taking hold of her and guiding her back indoors.

Mandy, a friend of Maggie's who works in Gatleys, suggested that they put a collecting tin on the counter to raise money for Wild at Heart – and they soon raised over £1,500 for the charity, which was incredible. They also started a scheme where people could donate things like blankets, beds, food and treats for rescue dogs, and the donations were unbelievably generous. Kind people flooded in to give away their unneeded kit. Some of it was given directly to Wild at Heart for the new animals they were bringing to the UK, and the rest we distributed around local animal shelters.

We've got another branch of Gatleys on the high street near where I live, and as soon as I park in town, Maggie's nose is in the air, sniffing away. We have to walk down the street and across a zebra crossing to get there, and she pulls me every inch of the way, only stopping to take in the aromas of the butcher's and the fish-and-chip shop.

Thanks to Maggie's ever-expanding profile, Wild at Heart approached me with the idea of doing a Maggie range of clothes, and I was overjoyed. I couldn't think of anything cuter than people walking around with pictures of Maggie on their tops, and all in such an incredible cause. Wild at Heart sent me some different images and suggestions of what we could use, and then an amazing artist and designer called Simeon Farrar came up with the overall look, including the wonderful "Love Is Blind" slogan. When they first told me they were going to use neon yellow on some of the designs, I really couldn't get my head around it. But they looked wonderful, and the bright colours really captured Maggie's radiant spirit. All of the clothes have got her story written on the back, which just makes it all the more special.

In the first week alone they sold over £5,000 worth of merchandise, and every last penny of the profits goes to the charity alone. I was so glad we had the opportunity to give back to the wonderful organisation that had brought Maggie into my life in the first place and transformed it for ever.

When people give a donation or buy something in aid of a charity, they're not just giving money – they're giving hope and making a difference. It's a chance not only to support the charity's work, but to spread the word even further when people wear their Maggie T-shirts and sweatshirts.

Wild at Heart have many recognisable faces on board. Pixie Geldof works closely with the charity, and is always happy to help out when they ask her, so she very kindly agreed to model the Maggie clothing line. She's a real animal lover, and she was also really interested to find out more about Mishka.

Emily Hunt, an Instagram influencer who fosters via Wild at Heart, also modelled the outfits, as did Mia Cecily, who also works with the foundation. We ended up doing the whole shoot in the middle of the street and the girls had to change outfits really quickly while we were snapping away.

The pictures were taken by a phenomenal photographer called Aidan O'Neill, who travels the world taking pictures and making films, and is very involved in supporting the foundation. Aiden volunteers for charity a lot. He was brilliant, because he just showed up, gave everyone very clear instructions, and then made room for me to stand behind him, using my failsafe trick of rustling a bag of treats so that Maggie would look at the camera!

CHAPTER NINETEEN
A WORLD AWAY

In September 2019, I joined a group of Wild at Heart volunteers travelling out to Lebanon, to see where it all began for Maggie.

It was a daunting prospect to visit a place where my beloved dog had been so cruelly treated, and where I knew there was a widespread problem with neglect and mistreatment of street dogs. The purpose of the Wild at Heart was to continue helping with the rescuing, rehoming and sterilising programmes that they already had in place. I knew that was an opportunity I could not turn down, as it would give me the chance to help the poor creatures out there who might otherwise be at risk of suffering the same terrible treatment that Maggie did.

We didn't want to go to Lebanon simply as finger-wagging Westerners trying to tell Lebanese people how things should be. What we wanted to do was to recruit more volunteers to lend a hand in the project, and to try and get some kind of infrastructure in place over there, so that dogs had somewhere safe to go temporarily before they were eventually rescued or fostered.

There was not an awful lot on offer for street dogs in Lebanon, because they were essentially seen as vermin thanks to the overpopulation problem. If Wild at Heart could raise enough funds, we hoped it would make the fostering or adoption process easier and more painless if homes were found for them in the UK. That visit was designed to be the first of many to ensure safer, better lives for Lebanese street dogs.

Another purpose of the trip was to contact existing charities out there and to see how they worked, so that we could find out more at first hand about life on the ground in Beirut. There were many amazing shelters like Give Me a Paw, BETA (Beirut for Ethical Treatment of Animals), and Mount Lebanon Dog Shelter already doing incredible work. I had already spoken to some people working at their shelters via Facetime or WhatsApp, but it was hugely beneficial to be able to meet them face-to-face, with a translator, and to see their facilities and learn more about their practices.

When we flew into Beirut, we were picked up by a lady called Alina, who works for BETA. Another gentleman called John Barret very kindly let us stay at his house in the hills. I was hugely excited about all I was going to experience and learn, especially as the trip had such a personal resonance for me. Everyone in the Wild at Heart team was wearing their "Love is Blind" Maggie T-shirts, and it felt like things had come full circle. In a sense Maggie was back in Lebanon once more, this time to help other street dogs.

I had decided that while I was in Lebanon, I wanted to try and get some firmer answers about was what really happened to Maggie when she lived here. So many conflicting stories had filtered through, and I wanted to try to separate fact from fiction. The general consensus when I got her was that Maggie had been attacked by children, shot at close range, and possibly also run over at some point. I wasn't sure if we'd ever know the full story, but I knew this was the best opportunity I'd ever had to find out.

Ultimately, it was wonderful to be able to see the place where Maggie used to live, and to get a sense of how things were for her. Maggie had become a bit of a celebrity even back in Lebanon. Everyone was so excited to hear about how she was doing, and the people we met in animal shelters asked me endless questions about her. It may sound strange, but I felt that seeing where she came from helped me to understand Maggie a little bit more.

Even though I sadly didn't get to meet the people who had actually rescued Maggie, I did meet some who had helped her on her journey. One woman told me how in the early days, Maggie would growl at people a lot. But she hadn't been blind for very long at that point and hadn't learnt to rely on her other senses, so she was probably just terrified.

I had felt nervous about going out to Lebanon and re-imagining what had happened to Maggie, but I was perhaps even more worried about seeing all the rescue dogs and becoming emotional at the state they might be in. I had already seen images of unimaginable cruelty online – I'd seen so many dogs in sorry states on rescue websites and animal charity pages. My biggest fear was that I would go out there and find a dog that was in desperate need, but that I wouldn't be able to help. I wanted to help them all.

It was my first time in the Middle East, and the people in Lebanon were so kind and hospitable. The BETA home was the first shelter we visited. There were around 800 dogs in total there, and when we pulled up I was greeted by a sight the like of which I'd never seen before in my life.

There were dogs *everywhere*.

The main BETA building is made up of concrete pens that used to hold pigs, but are now homes for the dogs. It was a surreal experience seeing so many hundreds of dogs running around an abandoned pig shelter. I would turn around to find 20 dogs gazing up at me, longing for affection, and then I'd turn the other way to find 20 more begging for a stroke or a cuddle.

Some dogs were in pens, and others were roaming free. There were no gates or fences keeping them contained, so they were free to leave at any time – but they never left, because they knew they would be fed at BETA, and they knew they were safe there.

The shelter was probably made up of about half mixed breeds and half pedigree dogs, but hardly any small dogs. They were mostly Maggie-sized or bigger. The pure-breeds must have originally been bred to be sold, but ended up being dumped, mutilated or abused for whatever cruel reason their owners came up with.

All the pedigrees were Leonbergers, German Shepherds, Caucasian Shepherds and huskies – really macho dogs.

There were a few Labradors, some Golden Retrievers and lots of Pit Bulls. Curiously, the Labradors and Golden Retrievers were the ones that weren't overly friendly, which is the total opposite of what we're used to in the UK.

One of our guides said there were so many stray huskies because a lot of people got them when they featured in Game of Thrones. In other words, they became "cool". It was devastating to see how such beautiful creatures could just be treated as trends that went in and out of fashion at the whim of their human owners.

I was astonished at how friendly all of the dogs were. A few barked because they were unsure of us at first, but they were just alerting us to their feelings rather than being aggressive. There were only about six dogs out of the 800 that seemed genuinely aggressive, and even then it was most likely just out of fear. Despite the hardships they had all faced, almost every dog was happy and waggy-tailed.

From a behavioural standpoint, though, this was the worst place a dog could be. The dogs were surrounded by concrete walls all day, and the highlight of their lives was when people like us went to visit. In the previous year, only 10 dogs from that shelter had been adopted in Lebanon, but thankfully some others had been flown out to the US and Canada, as well as the UK, to be rehomed.

When you adopt a dog from Lebanon, the money you pay covers their vet fees, papers and travel. Then if there ever is a little bit left over, which hopefully there will be, that will go towards helping other dogs in need.

And there were some dogs at the BETA shelter that were desperately in need. There was one poor German Shepherd dragging itself through urine and excrement because it had hip dysplasia. It was so sad to witness, but the people who run the shelter were determined to help it recover. They wouldn't turn any dog away, no matter what state it was in. But unsurprisingly, they didn't have the money to take them all to the vet and deal with their health issues.

They only managed to feed the dogs thanks to donations. It costs £10,000 a month to feed that many animals. The dogs are fed kibble, and a lot of it is very generously donated by a major retailer.

Despite all the amazing work BETA were doing, they struggled to support themselves and the shelter was barely fit for purpose. There were puppies running around everywhere, and dogs with missing legs. Some of the weaker dogs got picked on, not because the other dogs were mean – it was just because they were stressed, and their pent-up aggression led them to pursue the weaker ones.

The dogs were all very protective of their own areas and had become very territorial. To them, that filthy corner of an old pig pen was home. That was their space. Some of them didn't move from their "home" in case another dog stole it, so they sat inside all day guarding it, and would even do their business there.

There was a separate area for the Pitbulls, because sadly, their behaviour could be very unpredictable, and there were some dogs in there that had been used for fighting by humans in the past. They had had an aggressive mentality trained into them, so they also had to be kept apart from the other dogs. It wasn't their fault, poor things, it was just what they'd been taught.

I wasn't sure why so many aggressive dogs had ended up on the streets, but I could only assume they'd been bought for protection and then discarded by their owners when they were no longer needed.

The people in charge of the shelter did keep it remarkably clean, even though there were so many dogs (as well as some donkeys and cats!) and not all of them were toilet trained. It would be easy to judge the environment, but the people running the shelter were doing an amazing job all things considered, particularly given their lack of personnel and resources.

Some people might look at that shelter and think the dogs didn't look healthy, or that it couldn't be good for them being shut in a pen all day, but compared to what some of them had been through, it was a good life. And there was always the possibility of rescue, however slim, as the light at the end of the tunnel.

Many of the dogs at the BETA shelter will never get the chance to sit on a comfy sofa or get lovely treats. That's not the life they're going to have. But thanks to BETA, they do have people that look after them and feed them regularly, and the most important thing is that they're in good hands.

From what I witnessed, a lot of the dogs took solace and comfort in each other, and that helped me come to terms with the fact that some of them would be in that situation forever. There were some dogs that would be there for the rest of their lives, but they were living a decent life now, and they had their doggy friends there with them.

Besides, some of the before-and-after photos from BETA were breathtaking. It was a place full of amazing work, a place full of hope. One of the male dogs, Elko, who was due to come over to the UK soon, had been utterly transformed. At some point in the past he was a family pet, but somehow he found himself on the streets, and he survived on scraps for five years before he ended up at BETA. When he first went to the shelter his skin had been rubbed raw, and one of his front legs was so badly damaged it had to be amputated. In spite of his history, though, he was calm, stoic and deeply affectionate. As an older dog, all he truly wanted was a comfy couch to sit on, food in his belly and love in his heart. That's all any dog wants. I was so struck by Elko's before-and-after photos that I uploaded them on my Instagram page to celebrate the charity's achievements.

It was overwhelming seeing so many dogs in so many different states, but we had to put our own feelings aside and do what we could for the dogs while we were there. The first problem facing BETA was that their shelter was situated on land lent to them by a local farmer, but they'd effectively overstayed their welcome and he needed the land back. They were due to be kicked out soon, so were looking for somewhere to build a new shelter.

As far as I am concerned, any new animal shelter should be a long-term, no-kill shelter, so that any dog that is taken in there will safe. There are many shelters around the world that will take in dogs, and if they're not fostered or adopted within a certain timeframe, the dogs will be put down. It really doesn't bear thinking about. Animal shelters should be places of hope, not despair.

It's impossible to judge a dog's state of health just by looking at it. With street dogs, you have to check them up on a case-by-case basis. You can't assume anything from their appearance. When Maggie was first rescued, many people might have looked at her and thought there was no way she could survive. But just look at her now. She ended up being adopted, and she's happy now and lives a great life. If she'd been found by someone less caring and patient than Hussein, who knows what might have happened to her.

Some dogs can look ravaged on the outside, but can still have the capacity to live full and happy lives on the inside. Disfigurements are often superficial. Likewise, some dogs can look really healthy, but they might have terrible things going on internally and injuries that are invisible to the naked eye.

The day after visiting BETA, we met up with a man called Milo, who has a rescue shelter called Milo-AS (Milo Animal Shelter). He used to be in the army, but once day he had a kind of spiritual awakening and decided he needed to help animals in need. He left the army and took a complete change of career direction, setting up a rescue shelter instead. He gives everything he has to the dogs he looks after. I swear he would rather go hungry himself than let one of those dogs go hungry.

He lives in the countryside outside Beirut, and he goes out at 6am every morning to feed any stray dogs he finds. He drove us along his usual route and I asked him to stop the car because I saw a dog on the side of the road that I thought was unwell. Tragically, it was already dead. Somebody had snared it, so the poor thing had been caught by the foot, and had probably died from heat exhaustion, hunger or thirst. It was a horrible sight, and one that would be unthinkable in the UK.

At Milo's shelter, we met a purebred Belgian Malinois that had been poisoned. She had survived, but she was shaking constantly, so we called her Bambi because she was all wobbly. Nikki Tibbles later paid out of her own money to bring her over to the UK so that she could get help for her condition before finding her forever home. Her wobbles will get better over time, but in many ways the damage is permanent.

There was another little dog called Nina who had been run over, severely injuring her. Her back was broken during the accident – and yet she had managed to drag herself around for a month and find food and water. She was completely paralysed from the waist down, so the poor little mite had to drag herself along the road for a month hoping that someone would come to her aid. She travelled so far that she ended up with sores on her tiny, frail body. It was a heartbreaking story, but one that gave me hope. Milo had taken her under his wing and taken her to his foster shelter, where she got a bath, food, medical treatment and love – and also made new friends.

I had seen videos of her through Wild at Heart before we flew out to Lebanon. In them, she was only a few months old and I couldn't have said in all honesty that I was sure she was going to make it. But when I met her in person, she was six months old and a different dog altogether. She could run and play, scooting around on her temporary little handmade wheelchair, and she absolutely ruled the shelter. She was a proper power-house. She might not have been able to walk properly without a set of wheels, but she'd still put the dogs in their place if they were misbehaving. She certainly wasn't letting her disability hold her back. She was so happy zooming around on her wheels, and she ran over my toes too many times to count! She was stubborn, feisty and determined, and I loved her. I don't know what it is with these Lebanese dogs, but they all seem to be so resilient.

The plan was for her to get fixed up at the vet's, and after that I agreed to foster her for a while until she was ready to go to her new home. The great news was that she already had a new mum waiting in the wings. Her new owner saw her online and fell so madly in love with her that she made plans to move house just to accommodate Nina. She's moving to a bungalow just so that Nina will be able to get around more easily – because clearly stairs are going to be a bit of an issue.

Milo rescued another dog he called Runner, a German Shepherd cross. He picked him up off the side of the road and the poor thing was at death's door. He was so emaciated that all Milo wanted initially was simply to make sure that the dog had a peaceful death.

When I met Runner, he was so skinny that I could put my hands around his tummy. Can you imagine a German Shepherd being that thin? Milo used to have to have to pick him up to move him, and it took all the strength Runner had just to be able to hold his head up. He had no muscle mass or energy.

When you're that emaciated, your body only has enough resources to send information to your vital organs like your heart and your liver, so Runner's eyes stopped working and he was effectively blind. He probably couldn't hear very well either. He couldn't even see where his food bowl was, so Milo was having to hand-feed him every day.

Runner was getting more strength back every day, though, and since our visit he's started growling at people – which sounds bad, but is actually a really good sign because it shows that he's able to see and hear again. He reacts if people go near him when he's trying to eat, which is very common in street dogs who have been deprived of food or abused. When I met him I could tell that he was just a beautiful dog that had endured a really, really horrendous start in life.

The reason Milo called him Runner is because he was convinced he'll be able to go running with him one day, and I think he's absolutely right. Runner is now at the point where he can stand on his own, and soon he'll be strong enough to move around independently.

Milo is such an animal lover. He will help any living thing that's in need. He's basically like a grown-up version of 10-year-old me (without the exasperated dad). He once found a goat with a massive abscess on its back, which had become so infected that maggots were eating its flesh. He took it in and nursed it back to health. He even had an injured hawk at one point. He just wants to help these beautiful animals.

All in all, the trip was astonishingly positive, and a wonderful insight into the amazing work that is already being done to improve the living conditions of animals in Lebanon. Once we had more funding, Wild at Heart planned to start an education programme over there, to begin the long process of shifting attitudes towards animals as a whole. I'm always optimistic that things can change for the better and that we can teach people how amazing dogs can be. We can't change ingrained cultural attitudes overnight, but we can do our best. This would run alongside a widespread neutering programme, to help control the population and ensure there would be hope for every street dog we could get to.

Dogs and cats are adored pets in many households in Lebanon, just as they are here. There's a #dogsofLebanon hashtag to showcase the dogs that are cared for and loved, as local engagement with and support for animal rights grows and grows. Many Lebanese people are fighting the fight, campaigning for change and getting others to listen. They are determined to shift the country's reputation when it comes to animal cruelty.

It's easy to forget that it wasn't so long ago Lebanon endured a civil war, which devastated everything from human life to wildlife. It's understandable that when war broke out, animals went right to the bottom of the priority list. But 30 years on, the country is changing so much from day to day, and while they are still recovering in a lot of ways, there is significant rebuilding work going on. The fact that there are people over there who are trying to help animals when so much devastation has been inflicted so near to them is incredible.

I flew back home from Lebanon feeling much more uplifted than I thought I would. I felt like things were heading in the right direction. It was my first time visiting the country, but everyone I met there loved dogs and wanted to help.

I know it's a bit of a cliché, but even if we can save one dog from a life of misery, we have done good work. The

Wild at Heart Foundation has already saved numerous dogs and helped them to turn their lives around and find amazing homes, and it's essential that we continue that much-needed work.

Since I've been back home, about six people have sent me photos of Maggie of when she was still living in Lebanon, showing how she was passed along several times and people did their best to help her. It was heartwarming to know how much the efforts of animal rights activists and charities were already paying off.

The next step for Wild at Heart is to encourage more and more people in the UK to adopt from Lebanon, so as to relieve some of the pressure on the organisations out there.

The difficulty is the stigma around street dogs or rescues from other countries. Many potential fosterers worry about aggression or bad behaviour in street rescues from abroad. People often say they want to buy a dog as a puppy so they know what they're getting – but you can't always know, because behaviour depends on how you treat and train your dog, as well as its natural personality. In my opinion, there is no such thing as a bad dog – but there are plenty of bad owners.

I'm not naïve, and I know people will always want puppies for their cute factor. A lot of people want to know exactly where their dogs come from, and they want to meet the breeders to check that the dog is going to be healthy. That is understandable, and it is the best way for some people to go if they do not feel equipped to take on a rescue dog.

What is less understandable is the level of general concern about crossbreeds. Dogs crossbreed naturally, and the idea of a "pedigree" dog is a human invention, so the idea that if you buy a pedigree you "know exactly what you're getting" is a fiction. It upsets me that people turn their backs on dogs because they're not considered "perfect". Ultimately, breed has no impact on behaviour: whether you get pedigree or a mixture of an endless number of different breeds, if you love your dog and look after it, it will be happy and well behaved.

Another common misunderstanding about rescue dogs is the idea that they're a totally unknown quantity. If you rescue a dog from a shelter, the dog will have been assessed by experts at the shelter, so you will have a good idea of what you're getting. They will have considered the dog's needs and will know if it's good around children or other animals. It will all be there in writing. You will literally know what you're getting on paper.

There is a lot of fear around training street dogs, but it's no different to training any other kind of dog. Older dogs are just as capable of learning how to behave, and even things as basic as toilet training can be taught to more mature dogs. It's just a case of putting in some time and effort.

Any of the dogs you see on rehoming sites could be a Maggie. She, like all the other dogs I met in the shelters in Lebanon, is a lovely, lovely dog. And every one of those dogs deserves to be loved.

Love has to go both ways with animals. I know some people get dogs because they want love, but you have to give it back too. They will be amazing company for you, but equally, you have to think about their needs and provide for them.

There's a reason dogs have evolved with us over time. They just love you and want to be with you, and it's why more and more dogs like Maggie are going into care homes to comfort people. They understand us and we understand them. They are magical. They are the best thing in the world for people who are lonely.

A wonderful 85-year-old woman adopted an older Lebanese dog called Jenny, a beautiful little girl with a big underbite. When she took her in, I saw some cruel comments on Facebook saying it was unfair to give a dog to a woman who didn't have long left to live. Those people were completely missing the point. Age is irrelevant. Jenny now had a loving home, a social life, and happiness. She had nothing but four walls before. Besides, her new owner was fitter than a lot of younger people I know, and Wild at Heart had everything in place to help if anything did happen.

Every single rescue dog I know of that has come from Lebanon to the UK has found a fantastic new life, and has been wonderful. When dogs have been through so much, they must feel so relieved and grateful when they are finally rescued and looked after properly.

I have learnt so much about rescue dogs over the past five years. The last dog I bought was my Belgian Malinois cross, Biaroo, during my student years, but fostering and adoption is all I do now. I hope that by spreading the word about Maggie, people will become more understanding of street dogs and strays.

I found that once I knew the facts, I couldn't countenance going back. Once your eyes are open to the suffering that goes on around the world and what you can do to help, you can't close them again. You can't look away. Wild at Heart have called their latest campaign "Open Your Eyes" in honour of Maggie, and it's so fitting. I really did win the lottery with Maggie, but there are so many more utterly incredible dogs out there.

You may well ask why I went all the way to Lebanon to rescue a dog when we have dogs that need homes in the UK. My answer would be that in this country, we have better infrastructure to care for rescue dogs, whereas in Lebanon, as in many other countries, there is very little. Sometimes it takes people from elsewhere in the world to go and lend a hand. And while there are too many street dogs in Lebanon to manage, there is actually a lack of dogs in the UK, believe it or not. There aren't enough dogs. There is a shortage of rescues, and that's why so many people buy dogs instead.

In the UK, if you saw a dog running around the streets, the first thing you would wonder was where its owner was. In many other countries, the likelihood would be that they never had owners. We have so few street dogs in this country because most dogs are microchipped and account-ed for, and if they're not and they do end up stranded, they are few enough in number that they can be taken in and looked after. There are brilliant places like The Dogs Trust or the RSPCA who will make sure they're okay, and if they have injuries they will get the care they need.

That said, we're certainly far from perfect in Britain. You still hear horror stories of dogs abandoned by cruel people. Often they'll be dogs exploited for breeding that are no longer of use, or sometimes a pedigree dog will become pregnant by a dog of a different breed and the owner knows it will be harder to sell a mixed-breed litter, so that dog might get left by the side of the road. Some people are just out to make money out of whatever breed is in fashion, so the vicious cycle continues.

I am all for helping those dogs, as I am for helping any dog. But I also felt good about helping relieve the situation in a country without such extensive resources. I felt it was a responsible thing to do to step in and offer support from afar.

Ultimately, where you're born is a lottery, and there are also so many dogs around the world that need help. Some dogs are born in safe countries, where there are systems in place to help them, and others aren't so lucky. And there's little those dogs can do to help themselves.

Sometimes I tell people where I got Maggie from, they give me wary looks. "There are enough dogs over here that need help – why did you get one from another country?" I simply explain the important part of the story: that Maggie just needed help, and I was able to provide it.

If Roxanne and Wild at Heart hadn't intervened when they did, I have no idea what would have happened to Maggie or what position she would be in now. To the doubters, I would say that if you are concerned about the rescue dogs over here, by all means rescue one of them yourself or donate to your local charity. As long as you do something, you are helping the cause.

We have been incredibly lucky that people have been so kind supporting us with the Lebanon project. We've had wonderful donations and countless amazing messages. It may take a bit of time, but we will make the world a better place – one dishevelled street dog at a time.

CHAPTER TWENTY
MEETING THE ROYALS

I missed Maggie's birthday when I was out in Lebanon – I don't know when her official birthday is, so I celebrate it on the day when I first met her, 18 September. Birthday duties fell to my mum, who took her out for a little birthday party at a cafe in Steyning called Paws for Tea.

Maggie had a pupaccino, hot dogolate and pup cakes, and the lady who owns the café made her a cake and got her balloons. Her best friend Anne from the care home went along, and apparently no one stopped smiling all day.

Maggie's first summer of fame had flown by, and as autumn set in she received an exciting nomination for the Brave Britons awards – a very special honour for a very special dog. On 15 October 2019 Maggie, Mum and I travelled to London to attend the ceremony at the Army and Navy Club in Pall Mall. Maggie was nominated in the Hero

Pet category. The dog that won, Ethan, was from Brighton too – I was delighted my home town was so well represented! Ethan is a detection dog who can tell when his mum, Sally, is about to have a seizure, and warn her in advance. He's changed his mum's life, and he's yet another example of the amazing healing work animals can do. I felt like a winner just being in a room with all of those beautiful souls. Just to be included among them was an honour in itself.

There were so many inspiring people there who had done incredible things. We were sat at a table with a group of other people, and everyone got on really well. Maggie even had her own place card, with dog biscuits and water, which I thought was the sweetest thing. Everyone kept saying to me, "Maggie is so good, isn't she?"

What they didn't know is that she'd had a poo in Victoria train station just before we arrived.

We'd just got off the train and were walking down the concourse when she decided she needed to go. Poor Mags obviously didn't know whether she was inside or outside because it's pretty blustery on those platforms, and she must have thought we were walking down the street.

We were just walking up to the ticket barrier when she squatted down and did her business there and then. When a girl's got to go... Thankfully there weren't that many people around, and I picked it up and got rid of it before I got too many horrified looks.

We were sat across the table from a boy of only eight years old, who had steered his mum's car into a layby after she had a seizure at the wheel while they were travelling at 60 miles an hour. He also won a Pride of Britain award, and he so deserves it. There was also a lovely old man who is the world's oldest bagpipe player. He was in his 90s, so it was pretty hard for him to have enough puff to play. When the Duke of Kent walked in, he looked at him and said, "I'm sorry, your majesty." He felt the need to apologise because he wasn't quite as in tune as he wanted it to be. It was so cute.

It was such a fun day and it was amazing to meet so many incredible people. The big winner was an amazing 15-year-old girl called Ellie Challis, AKA the Mighty Minnow. She lost her lower legs and both of her hands to meningitis when she was just 16 months old, and initially learnt to swim so she could be safe in the water. But while on holiday in Florida, she was inspired by the resilience of a bottlenose dolphin called Winter, who lost his tail after being caught up in a fishing net. Ellie had one of those "if he can do it, so can I" moments. Fast forward to today and she's now an award-winning Paralympic swimmer and in training to be a para snowboarding champion too.

Maggie got to have her photo taken with Simon Weston, who was presenting the awards, which was wonderful. He was so nice to her. She also even got to meet the Duke of Kent, who is the Queen's Cousin – my scrappy little street dog got to meet royalty! I could never have imagined that happening. Her life truly is rags to riches. Or maybe Mags to riches? Anyone?

Mum and I had found ourselves in unfamiliar surroundings at such a posh dinner, and one of the funniest moments of the day was when she picked up the wrong jug from the table and mistakenly put custard in her coffee instead of milk. Even though she realised her mistake with a visible laugh and a groan, Mum had to style it out and drink the coffee anyway, even though it had curdled.

Those kinds of events might not be my sort of thing, but they are still lovely to go to every now and again. I'm much more comfortable out walking in a field with a beanie hat on, but when the opportunity arises it's wonderful to dress up and have lovely food and get a bit spoilt. It was a very loud awards ceremony, and people messaged me on Instagram afterwards asking me if Maggie was afraid of the noise, but it didn't seem to bother her at all. I would never have taken her if I thought for a second it would have a negative effect on her. To her, it's just normal life. She'd be much more concerned if she wasn't the centre of attention!

Occasions like those are just some of moments when I've been able to step back and see how much love Maggie has around her. I wonder if she knows. This funny little street dog who was ignored and pushed aside for so long is suddenly right in the spotlight. She finally has the love and praise she deserves.

When I first got her, I thought the things she'd want most out of life were a comfortable sofa, food to eat and lots of love, all of which I could give her. I thought maybe I could fix her and send her on her way, or that she would be happy to settle for a quiet life. How wrong I was!

I had never envisaged all of this. I could see what an inspiration she was to so many people. Even if she didn't know it, what mattered was that people were moved by her and she was changing their worlds a little bit. She might have been blind herself, but she was opening people's eyes to the idea of being different and being okay with it. I understood that she was a lesson to us all in confidence and absolute self-acceptance.

Against all expectations when she first arrived, Maggie had also become a lesson to other dogs in exemplary behaviour. When we returned to the Wildlife Drawing event one year on from our first outing, the change in my girls in the space of just a year was plain for all to see. Maggie had gone from being an overexcited ball of chaotic energy to a calm, confident dog, still energetic and sociable, but respectful and obedient too. Mishka, who had previously been so shy and nervous, was now running around and bounding up to people, wanting to say hello to everyone. I actually had to apologise for her being *too* friendly. I'm sure a lot of her development was courtesy of Maggie too. Mishka also helps Maggie out if she gets nervous of other dogs, and she acts a bit of a bodyguard if she senses that Maggie is worried. They balance each other out really well, and I'm so glad I held my nerve in those tricky early days. My girls became the perfect pair.

Aside from pooing on station platforms, the only thing I still had to tell Maggie off for now and again was rummaging through the bin. At some point she clearly taught herself the art of bin diving, and there were no small number of occasions when I came home to find rubbish all over the floor.

The tricky thing about this final part of her training, though, was that I could never tell Maggie off unless I caught her in the act. If you come home and your sofa has been chewed to pieces, there's no point in telling the dog off – at that point it's already forgotten and moved on. Unless you actually catch them doing something, it's pointless trying to punish them. If you're angry with your dog hours after it's done something bad, it won't associate being told off with the naughty thing it's done. Dogs aren't smart enough to know that you're upset about something they did that morning – they're too busy living in the moment.

The funny thing was, Maggie always dobbed herself in. If I came in to find her rolling on the floor and licking her lips – a sign she was upset and nervous – I'd know instantly what she'd been up to. I purposefully didn't get annoyed with her. I'd usually laugh and say, "Oh no, has the fox been in the kitchen again, Maggie?"

CHAPTER TWENTY-ONE
BEAUTIFUL BELLA

Just when I thought my home life couldn't get any more hectic, I was asked to foster a lovely dog called Bella, another rescue from Lebanon. Ironically, I had just taken myself off all the fostering websites and social media pages – I had decided to take a bit of a break while I got my business properly up and running again. But baby Bella had other ideas, and when Wild at Heart contacted me and said they had a dog that needed me, my head said "No!" but my heart screamed "Yes!"

The only thing we knew about Bella was that she had been thrown out of a second-floor balcony when she was a puppy, and both of her front legs had been broken. Neither of her legs had set properly: her left leg was set at a 90° angle and her right leg was also turned out, so she looked like she had ten to two feet. As if that wasn't bad enough, she had awful sores on her paws, which made it even harder for her to walk.

She was found in a shelter, but she was living in such horrific conditions she probably would have been better off on the streets. Injured dogs and puppies were quite literally being left to rot as their wounds became infected.

Bella fell pregnant at least once in the shelter. She only had two puppies, who sadly didn't make it. The size of her litter shows how deficient in nutrients she must have been, because normally dogs of her physical size have litters of around six to eight puppies.

Thankfully Bella had been taken in by Milo, so she was fed well and cared for while Milo started exploring the options for her. He contacted Roxanna at Wild at Heart to see if she could help Bella get over to the UK, and Roxanna made the necessary arrangements. It took three months to get her over to the UK, but it was so worth it.

Bella was adopted when she first came over to the UK, but the people who took her in decided she was too much to deal with and threatened to have her put down. I couldn't stand the thought that she had been through so much, from breaking her legs to moving to another country and finally finding her family, only to die here or be sent back to Lebanon.

That was the point at which I stepped in and offered to foster her. I would take her in, heal her up, and then we could find her a new home with people who would appreciate what a gorgeous girl she was.

I collected Bella from Clacket Lane services, and she just jumped straight into my van and gave me a look as if to say, "I guess I'm coming to live with you now then." She seemed almost resigned to it. She had been so used to moving around that it didn't seem to bother her.

She was very sweet and loving from day one. But I understood why her first family in the UK found her hard to look after, especially if they hadn't had any previous experience looking after dogs in need of a lot of extra care. In many ways, fostering Bella was like taking on an out-of-control toddler. Bella had never been taught right and wrong. She didn't know how to behave in a home, because she had never had one. It was a case of starting again and helping her to learn as if she'd only just come into the world. How on earth is a dog supposed to know what they should and shouldn't do if they've never been shown? She was in survival mode, following the examples of the other street dogs.

Bella had separation anxiety, so I had to crate train her as I do all my foster dogs. If she wasn't crated when I went out, I was guaranteed to come back to a protest wee or poo. If I didn't shut her crate properly at night, Bella would get out and go for a wander, and I woke up one morning to a poo on my couch. I was not happy. Those are the joys of fostering.

She didn't know how to signal that she wanted to go outside to go to the toilet, and it took her a long time to realise that if she went and stood by the door I would open it for her and she could do her business where she was supposed to do her business! I had nearly two months of her squatting down wherever she fancied and just letting it all out – so she wasn't the kind of dog I could take round to visit people. The poor girl had been used to sitting in her own filth when she was a street dog, so she didn't know the polite way to do things. That was her life for so many years that it took time for her to internalise new habits. She was very set in her ways, and I had to show her there was a different way to do even the most basic things.

But she was a responsive and instinctive dog, and she picked up a lot on what Maggie and Mishka did. Eventually she realised they always ask to go outside to use the "toilet", and she followed suit. That was a good day in our house.

Like so many rescue dogs, Bella was hyper-responsive to food, and was uncontrollable around it. She got so excited when I gave the dogs their dinner that she started jumping up, even though her damaged legs really couldn't take the strain. She was so desperate for food after being malnourished on the streets that she was willing to put her chronically painful legs at risk for a meal. At first, I had to plate up all the dogs' food out of her sight in my van, before walking it into the house and serving it to them it in the calmest way possible.

Maggie and Mishka were happy to eat together by now without any problems, but I put Bella in her crate at dinner time so she knew she was safe and no one would try to steal her kibble and veg. The shelter she was in had been so bad that the dogs were fighting each other for scraps, so it's no wonder her issues with food had been so exacerbated. Maggie and Mishka were generally really good about their food because they're so used to having other dogs around. But I just knew that Bella would wolf down her food and then start on Maggie and Mishka's if she got the chance – and I found it hard keeping weight on slender Mishka already.

Bella learnt basic commands really well, though. If she went near the girls' meals and I looked at her and said "no", she'd retreat and sit down quietly. I knew without a doubt that I would be able to train her to be totally comfortable around food, because eventually she would realise that there was always another meal coming. But I had to take it slow, and take sensible precautions in her training.

I always loved working with my dogs and teaching them new tricks and games, but I had to minimise how much of that I did with Bella. When she was having fun she tended to forget how much pain she was in, and then she really suffered later.

When I first took her out for walks I would always keep her on the lead, but she was desperate to belt off after rabbits and squirrels like the other pooches. It was so unfair that she couldn't join in the hunting, not that they have ever caught a single thing between them. But if ever she did overdo things, that night she would lie down and lick her paws, and her little face was heart-rending.

I needed to find ways to keep Bella stimulated and stop her getting bored, without her exerting herself too much physically. So I came up with brain games for Bella and me to do inside the house to keep her occupied. I bought her puzzle balls, frozen Kongs and a Kong Wobbler, and whenever I gave her treats I would put them inside the Kong Wobbler and it took her ages to work out how to get it out.

Maggie and Mishka very kindly let her use their own brain game, a giant piece of plastic where you had to move things around and pick things up to get the treats hidden underneath. I also had a wooden one with bones that Bella had to knock off the top. Then she had to slide panels away to get to the treats, so it was a good challenge. She was brilliant at that straight away, proving how smart a dog she was.

Maggie and Mishka both love brain games, so they had a great time with Bella. Dogs love exploring and learning new things. A lot of dogs can count: they always know how many treats you give them! Lolli can count her tennis balls. If I take five balls out with me on a walk and I throw them all, she'll fetch them, but if she only retrieves four she'll go back out and look for the fifth.

Dogs are so much smarter than people think. It's generally thought that their intelligence is the same as a child of about two to two and a half, but it definitely varies. I've met some dogs that act as if they have the mental age of a five-year-old – they remember everything – and I've met other dogs like lovely Lennard, who doesn't know whether he's coming or going half the time. Sometimes even remembering to put one paw in front of the other seems like an effort, though he can get away with it because he's so handsome.

Because it was tough for Bella to walk, I began taking her swimming, which was much gentler on her legs. I took her to local streams and rivers, and I would put my oldest leggings on and get in with her. We would do a swim-walk and she would go with the tide. She was so in love with food that I could easily lure her in with treats, but once she was in the water swimming away, she was pretty happy.

It was good for building up strength in her legs, but it wasn't putting anywhere near as much pressure on them as running or walking was. Ideally, she would have gone to hydrotherapy, but it costs a lot of money, and it wasn't fair to go back to the charity and ask for help with that, so we made do and improvised.

The swimming helped Bella to get rid of some of the build-up of energy and anxiety she suffered from. She's supposed to be an active dog, so it was like the equivalent of making a very active person sit around on their backside for weeks, doing nothing. It would get to you, because exercise is crucial to mental health. It's not just good for your body – it's good for your brain too, as exercise releases the feel-good hormone serotonin.

I saw a physical and emotional change taking place in Bella. When she came to live with me at first, she would never look me in the eye. She might look at me and then look away really quickly, but she could never hold my gaze. It was like she was always afraid I was going to tell her off. Even if I moved my hand too quickly, she would yelp presumably because she thought I was going to hit her. But soon enough, when I put her collar on she would lie on the floor and put her legs in the air because she was happy. The bond between us grew strong in a short space of time. I saw her change from a nervous, fearful, sad dog into a joyful one.

Because of Bella's leg problems, however, I always knew she would need an operation at some point. Surprisingly, the issue in her legs wasn't all in the joints or bones – it was a build-up of arthritis.

To do the procedure, the charity had to get approval from a vet, and the first vet we spoke to said it might be better to put her down. But eventually we found one who was willing to take a chance on baby Bella.

We knew that if the first operation on her left leg was a success, she was pretty much in the clear. We would then be able to operate on her right leg to correct the issues she had with that one, which were far less severe. She was with me for almost three months before the surgery, and it was always going to be a bit of a gruesome op.

The vet broke her left leg, straightened it and then put a custom-made metal plate inside it. It was a lengthy procedure, and she had to spend two weeks at the vet while she recovered. Every day was so tough, knowing that Bella was probably in agony. I still had my other two noisy girls at home, but the house did feel quite empty without her. It was an emotional time.

There was so much swelling from the surgery that they had to open up the back of Bella's leg to allow the skin to stretch. Their biggest fear was that the skin wouldn't join up again, leaving a gap that wouldn't be able to heal properly. If that was the case, they were unsure whether or not they would be able to amputate, considering her right leg also had a lot of issues. There was a question mark over whether she would be able to walk at all, and therefore whether she would have any quality of life at all. Horrifyingly, that meant we also had to have a conversation about whether it would be fair to keep her alive if the first operation failed.

The veterinary nurses had to change her bandage every day, and it took two nurses to hold her down because it was so uncomfortable. When she was eventually allowed home, I had to change her bandages daily, and she cried and whimpered every time. I felt terrible, but I knew it was the least I could do for her. The first time I changed a bandage, it took me two hours. I used a tiny pair of nail scissors so I could be as gentle as possible, but it was still so painful for her.

I was planning on two weeks of bed rest and plenty of treats for Bella, with nurses Maggie on Mishka on hand to dish out get-well cuddles. However, things didn't run that smoothly.

One night, Bella must have been irritated by her leg, so she somehow managed to get her protective cone off by rubbing it against her case, and she started chewing at the bandages and then licking the skin underneath, which meant an emergency visit to the vet the following day.

Her wound had already become infected, and when the vet did a swab test he discovered that it contained a fungus of a kind he had never seen in a dog before. It was sometimes found on the skin of humans, and somehow it had transferred into Bella's leg and wouldn't stop growing. They couldn't figure out why, and it was also antibiotic-resistant, so the pressure was on to prevent her from getting very sick, very quickly. She was a medical mystery, and it was so scary knowing that she only had a 50-50 chance of survival.

The only way to treat her was using fungus medication and intravenous antibiotics – a very expensive process. The operation cost a fortune, and the Wild at Heart Foundation team made the call on the next steps, and whether or not we could continue with her treatment.

Waiting for them to decide what was best for Bella, assess their finances and confirm whether they could afford further treatment was one of the worst periods of my life. I knew they were desperate to help, but any money that comes in to the charity very quickly gets swallowed up helping dogs in need.

I had a really strong feeling they would come through and find the money from somewhere, but there was always that chance that the money just wasn't there.

Thankfully, Wild at Heart came back and said that the funds had been cleared, and as well as their amazing contribution, we also got donations from some very kind dog lovers. After that, all I could do was pray Bella would pull through and fight off the infection attacking her leg.

She had to have four operations in the end, and incredibly, the vet waived the fees of the last two ops because he wanted Bella to have to the best chance of survival, and he didn't want money to be the issue that cost her her life.

Bella began her recovery from the infection, but because the specially made plate that had been fitted in her leg had to be removed when the infection took hold, she had to have a strange-looking cage contraption fitted instead to keep her bone in place. It wasn't the most aesthetically pleasing thing you've ever seen, but as long as it did the job, what did it matter? On 12 December my girl was finally home, and I was over the moon.

When Bella got home she had to sleep in a gigantic plastic travel crate so there was room for her, her cone *and* her leg cage. She had metal pins in her leg, and there was a danger they could get caught in the bars of a wire cage, so plastic was definitely the safest option.

The infection was on its way out, but she had to take another two weeks of antibiotics, before having physio and seeing the vet weekly to keep an eye on her progress. She needed one last surgery to fuse her humerus bone to the leg with a tiny plate, and then it would be time to make a call on her other leg.

Whatever happened in future, I couldn't wait to see her running around, free of pain. She was about to start a whole new life and enjoy the things she couldn't as a puppy.

She had been such a brave girl throughout. She'd been on multiple tablets a day at some points, and she wasn't always great at taking them, but the cheese and peanut butter trick worked a treat, as ever!

I knew Bella was properly on the mend when she joined in a howling session with Mishka. Later the same day when I was carrying her through the kitchen, she stuck out her tongue and tried to lick my dinner which I'd left on the counter. Clever girl!

I can understand people questioning why I foster dogs when it can be so upsetting. The answer is that I foster them so that these forgotten dogs can get the second chance they deserve. I train them, I nurse them, I love them, I feed them, and they finally get the opportunity to know that they are safe.

Then once they're all fixed up and ready to be adopted, I cry like a baby as I wave them off. The tears are a real mix of happiness and sadness, but my heart feels so full when I know that a previously unloved or uncared for dog is going to have a happy life.

I couldn't put a number on how many animals I've rescued in my life. I've always swooped in and helped any animal that looks like it's in need or injured, and I'll carry on until the day I die.

I've got a pet rat called Morty now, who has added to our animal family. I was talking to a woman who works in one of my local pet shops and was saying that I wanted to get a rescue rat, and by total coincidence their vet department had just had one handed in. It was fate! I made a donation and took him straight back home to meet the girls – don't worry, I got him a very secure cage.

I could see Mishka's eyes light up when I walked in the door with him. I kept catching her staring at the cage, whereas Maggie went up and gave him a sniff and a friendly lick and then left him alone. Morty is a cheerful little thing. Rats are sociable creatures, so it's nice for him to be around other animals, even if one of them would love to eat him.

People ask how I deal with saying goodbye to animals I care for. My honest answer? I get all of my emotions out, and I don't care what anyone thinks. It doesn't bother me if a total stranger thinks I'm weird when I start crying while talking about my dogs, and sometimes when I'm at home hugging Maggie and Mishka I will just feel an overwhelming need to cry to find release. I never hold myself back. I think *not* crying is one of the worst things we can do. Holding emotions down is only preventing the inevitable. If I need to cry, I cry wherever I am.

I really do think fostering is good for the soul. It can be tough, because you fall in love with every foster dog and you want to keep them, but I know from the word go that I can't. Sadly, I just don't have a big enough home for all the dogs I foster, so it is my job to patch them up and send them on their way to have a lovely life with someone new. Once one foster dog has flown the nest, I'm usually preparing myself for a new foster dog to come my way, so I'll start putting my energy into that.

I keep in touch with a lot of the owners of dogs I have fostered, but I never feel like I have any sense of ownership over them, and I don't expect anything from the people that adopt them. I love receiving photos and updates, but equally I'm just a halfway house for the dogs, so once they leave my care I have to accept that they belong to someone else.

When I see a dog running around happy and being loved there is no feeling like it, and that is why I am able to love the dogs and then let them go. It's amazing to think back on helping to make that happen.

I always take a photo of myself with every foster dog before they go to their new home so that I have that memory of them, but other than that it's a case of letting them fly free and enjoy their wonderful new lives.

When I get old and forgetful, I plan to have a massive scrapbook with photos of all the dogs I've fostered and helped over the years, so I can remember them all. I'm going to have such incredible memories to look back on, and I feel so lucky.

CHAPTER TWENTY-TWO
A WAGGY ENDING

When I reflected back over Maggie's incredible year since she came to the UK, I realised that she:

- Gained 270,000 followers from all around the world (and even more now!)
- Helped raise money for other street dogs just like her.
- Appeared on prime-time television – twice!
- Was nominated for multiple awards.
- Made more friends than I could count.
- Met royalty.
- Appeared in numerous magazines and newspapers.
- Became a registered therapy dog.
- Helped Mishka with her confidence.

- Took part in several photo shoots.
- Appeared in a fashion show.
- Made countless people smile and shed tears of joy.

Not bad, huh?

There were plenty of excitements to round off 2019, an amazing year for Maggie and me. First, we had heaps of fun shooting Maggie's 2020 calendar. It was created by Lucy Reeve, an amazing photographer who works with Wild at Heart, and who came up with all the ideas and got all the props together. There was a picture of Maggie with an ice-cream that was actually made of foam, but it was amazingly crafted and looking very realistic. We had to put peanut butter on the back of it to make Maggie lick it, of course.

Then, at the end of the year, I decided to get a DNA test done for Maggie. I wouldn't never know the full story of what happened to Maggie – only she knows that – but it felt like a lovely way to complete the fullest picture I could form of her past and her present.

A company called Wisdom Panel carried out the test for us, combing through all of Maggie's genetic markers to find out her backstory. Knowing what breeds she was didn't make a huge difference to me, because Mags is who she is and that's why I love her. But it did somehow make me feel that little bit closer to her – if that was possible!

The DNA test revealed that Maggie is 25% Anatolian Shepherd, 25% German Shepherd, 12.5% German Wirehaired Pointer, and 37.5% who the hell knows. And 100% superhero, obviously.

The results didn't come as a surprise to me. I always knew she was going to have German Shepherd in her, but having been out to Lebanon and seen how many Pitbulls there were, I wondered if she had a bit of Pitbull in her. I was a little concerned about it, because Pitbulls are a banned breed in this country.

It was fascinating to find out which breeds came from which side of her family. The Anatolian Shepherd and German Shepherd both came from her father's side – so his parents were purebred German Shepherd and Anatolian Shepherd.

Maggie being part Anatolian Shepherd makes perfect sense because, in the nicest possible way, they are big idiots. They're really dopey, loving dogs, and Maggie has those traits in abundance. They also have big barks

– and Maggie has a *giant* bark. It's the same with German Shepherds. They are such friendly, lovely dogs, though they are also really bright (I do worry Maggie might have slightly missed out there).

On her mum's side, it was mutts all the way. There were so many different breeds in her that there was no way of pinpointing the exact types of dog, or the number of different ones. Judging by the DNA test, Mags' mum came from a long line of feral dogs.

My theory was that Maggie's dad was owned by somebody, but he went out for a roam and had a bit of a frisson with Maggie's mum. Maggie (and her siblings, if she had any) were the result.

One of the most incredible things about the DNA test was finding out what colour eyes Maggie had before she was blinded. Amazingly, the test could pinpoint her eye colour, so I found out that Maggie had brown eyes when she was younger. I can imagine her having light brown eyes like a German Shepherd. I imagine they were a piercing orangey-brown, because she's such a pretty lady.

It's crazy to think that when I first fostered her, some people thought Maggie was so damaged she should have been put down. Just look at her now! She is proof that anything is possible. If you'd told me two years ago that I would have a disabled dog who would become so well-known we'd be invited to appear on prime-time TV shows, I would have laughed my head off.

I feel so lucky that we have met so many amazing people along the way as Maggie has transitioned from cowering street dog to super-confident diva. Every single person she has met has played a role and helped her. Even if you've simply liked one of her posts or given her a little stroke, it's all made a difference.

It makes me burst with pride that she's capable of doing so much. If I were her and had been through what she has, I think I would have given up a long time ago.

But then, would I? I think, deep down, we are all stronger than we know. All it takes is a little love and support from someone to show us that. Despite everything Maggie has been through, she loves, she trusts and she cares. And if that isn't an amazing reason to be more Maggie, I don't know what is.

Whoever it was who tried to break her spirit and take her life from her, they failed. Maggie's spirit is simply indestructible. She has suffered more than any living soul ever should, and yet she has found it in herself to forgive, move on and live her best life. To be able to trust people again when that trust was challenged time and time again is just unbelievable.

Maggie takes everything in her stride, because she's had to handle so much in such a short amount of time. I think people sometimes forget how young she is (we can't be certain, but vets estimate she's between four and five at the time of writing). She's been through an incredible amount for a dog of her age. In fact, for a dog of any age. I think that's what's made her so resilient and fearless now.

These days Maggie leads the way. She storms around, making people happy and loving life. She will walk at heel if I tell her to, but generally she's right out front showing the world what she's got.

I was asked to write a 250-word piece for the Paaw House charity about how Maggie has affected me, and inevitably it took me about five hours because I could not stop crying. I would write a few words and then bawl my eyes out and have to stop. Once I felt strong enough I'd start again. It was like the best but worst therapy ever. When you stop and think how much your dog has done for you, it can be overwhelming. I think there are times when people seek out dogs without really knowing why

– or they come to you when you need them. Sometimes you don't realise how much you needed them at the time until you look back.

This is the piece I wrote, word for word.

There are a hundred different ways to explain how Maggie has impacted my life – to condense them into an article is a difficult task. She has influenced my mental health, social life and physical health without question. She also loves me with a love so pure I can't imagine anyone loving me like she does. These things are not unique to Maggie, it's just what dogs do. It's why we love them unconditionally. What's unique to Maggie is that she has restored my faith in humans.

Throughout my life I have been brought down by those I loved the most. I lost my faith in humanity and shut myself away so I couldn't be hurt anymore. Then Maggie came and changed my understanding of my world.

Here was a dog who had been abused, tortured and mutilated. Her eyes pulled out, her ear cut off, her jaw fractured, her body shot with a shot gun, littering her tiny body with hundreds of pellets... all this while heavily pregnant. Here was a dog that should have died, yet she survived. She should have given up on the world, but she didn't. She should have hated humans for all the pain they caused her, and yet she had forgiven. If this little dog could learn to love again, then so could I.

She reminds me daily of lessons that I once knew but had forgotten. Things your parents teach you as a child. She taught me to be kind, love unconditionally and forgive. I offered to foster Maggie for one reason – because it was the right thing to do. She needed me and I now I know how much I needed her. That one act of kindness has changed my life and now affects hundreds of thousands of others. Maggie's story of love and forgiveness impacts each person she meets, but most importantly her love has given my once lonely life a new and greater purpose.

—Mum of @maggiethewunderdog

Mishka brought so much love into my life and changed my world. And then Maggie came along and flipped it on its head. I've met so many new people via my girls, and every weekend I'm doing something new and meeting people from every walk of life. It really is a crazy life with Maggie, and I never know what to expect.

I want to carry on doing things that make Maggie and Mishka happy. I want to travel much more with them both. I'd love to put them in the back of the van and go on a trip around Europe. It would also be wonderful if I could take the dogs to America to meet some of my family, and to meet some of the people we've become friendly with via Instagram.

There are so many people around the world that I talk to every day, and we've formed really firm friendships even though we're miles apart and we've never met. I would love to take the dogs on a tour – a friendship tour!

I want Maggie to see the world. I know that sounds a little ridiculous because she can't *see* as such, but she will feel the world and she will smell it, and she will know where she's been because she'll feel it with her heart.

My life has been a million times better since I got my two beauties. I really feel like I hit the jackpot. The world feels like a happier place to me now. It's strange for me to think back on, because all of this has come out of sad situations, but ultimately, they've ended up bringing endless joy to me and to the world.

Even if I wake up and I don't feel great, or I've got things going on in my life that are tough, I just have to look at my girls and everything feels better. If I am in a bad mood or I'm stressed, you can guarantee one of the girls will come over and give me a hug and make me feel better again. There's nothing quite like waking up to wagging tails, and knowing that you're going to bring happiness to your dog's day, and they're going to do the same for you.

People think I'm crazy because I don't go on holiday – I would much rather spend time with the dogs. Honestly, given the choice between hanging out with my dogs or lying on a beach, I'll hang out with the dogs every time. They bring sunshine into my life. They may not be perfect in everyone's eyes, but they're perfect for me. They keep me sane and humble, and I am grateful for them every single day. They have changed my life for the better in every possible way.

I want my Maggie and Mishka to live forever. The other day I had a really good cuddle session with them and I got this overwhelming feeling of sadness that there will be a time when I won't be able to wake up to their terrible morning breath and licky kisses. I know it's irrational to think like that, but I cannot imagine a world without them. Nobody will ever love you more than a dog. There's a reason they're called man's (and woman's!) best friend.

Maggie and I have both finally found a place where we fit in. I have always been the crazy dog lady, and Maggie's always been the dog that's different, but we've found where we belong and what we're here for – and that's making other people happy. Look how much we've done together already. She's helped me to find "my people".

When we go to events together, I meet people just like me. I meet people who love dogs more than anything, who also cry every time they talk about them, and who want to make a difference for dogs around the globe. For once, I don't feel like the odd one out.

Maggie is perfectly imperfect, and her flaws make her what she is. She has the cutest snaggle tooth because of the way her jaw sits. Her lips and nose are wonky, and she has funny fur swirls on her bum that wiggle when she walks. But those things don't define her – they are just who she is. When she walks, she walks with pride. Maggie could not be happier about how she looks and who she is.

So many of us look in the mirror and only see our flaws. Our hair won't feel right, we'll think we look tired, or we'll question if we've put on a few pounds. I love that Maggie does not care about any of those things. Some days her hair is sticking up all over the place like someone's tried to backcomb it.

Is she bothered? What do you think?

She never looks tired, and as for her weight? Maggie had just as much sass when she was a larger lady, and if she did ever put on weight, she would just think there was more of her to love.

I'm very lucky to have amazing people around me, and my dogs would never judge me on what I wear or the fact that I never wear a scrap of make-up. They don't care – they love what's inside of me more than anything. Hell, Maggie doesn't even know what I look like!

Maggie can't see people on the outside, so she loves what's on the inside. Imagine if we humans could do the same? They say love is blind, and in Maggie's case that couldn't be more true.

I feel the same about Maggie. How she looks makes her stand out in a crowd, but she is unique as opposed to weird. She is wonky but beautiful, and she knows better than anyone that how fancy your car is or how many designer bags you own does not say anything about who you are as a person. We're all perfectly us when we choose to be. Maggie was overlooked and considered to be undesirable because of her differences, but perfection is a myth. Who decides when someone is good enough or not? Sometimes something as ridiculous as a trend can be a marker for whether someone or is in or out. But being a kind, decent human being is the only trend we should care about being a part of.

I really hope Maggie makes people feel that it's okay to be different, and that you should be proud of who you are.

I've fostered and looked after so many dogs over the years, and I've never met a dog like her. Despite all her pain, she loves people so much. It's not normal for a creature like her to be so positive and energetic when she's been through so much, but she is proof that we can all overcome our issues with a bit of love and support.

One of my friends said to me recently that all they see when they look at Maggie now is a beautiful dog. They don't see her flaws. I feel exactly the same. What would you see if you saw Maggie walking down the street? Would you think she was an abused, depressed dog, or would you think she was a happy, carefree pup enjoying a stroll with her owner? Most of the time, people will walk right past her and not have a clue that she's different, and that's a testament to how far she's come.

And what about the future? My main plan is to win the lottery so I can open The Wunder Dog Centre for Wonky Dogs, where loads of rescue dogs can come and live. Stressed-out people can pay to come and cuddle them, so I can continue to keep them in the style to which they will become accustomed. There won't be any need to pay hundreds of pounds to a counsellor – just come and hang out with pooches, and all will be okay!

Failing that, I would like to buy a piece of land and be a halfway house for animals that need fixing up before they move on. I have to work out a way to be able to do that financially, but that's my ultimate goal.

I would happily give up everything to be able to own a rescue centre for animals. I still have to work out how, but there has to be a way for me to do it. It truly would be my perfect job to take all the dogs that are broken and fix them up before sending them on their way. Mishka and Maggie would love it, because they'd have new friends all the time.

Aside from that, we are still going for gold in the training and aiming for Crufts. I want to show that Maggie is just as good as any other dog.

When I look back at photos of Maggie before she came to the UK, it's like looking at a totally different dog. I know the dog in the before photos *are* Maggie, but when I compare them to how she looks now that she's been fed on love, good food and long walks, it feels like a miracle.

I'm sure Maggie feels like the luckiest dog in the world. Lucky that she was rescued, lucky that she has so many friends (she has a much better social life than I do!), lucky that she has a mum and sister who love her so much, and lucky that she gets to smell freedom and comfort when she wakes up every day. And of course, Mishka and I are and all the people that get to hang out with magical Maggie are just as lucky.

From the bottom of my heart, thank you to all of you who have taken Maggie into your hearts. I am humbled every day when I read comments on social media, and I get so emotional knowing that so many people care about her. Who knew that a little dog could have such a big effect on people?

Thank you for helping to spread her message of love, acceptance and joy, and for sharing her unique story with others so that they can do the same. I hope Maggie's photos bring happiness to people if they're having a bad day, or that they can make a good day even better.

My mum once asked me what Maggie means to me, and I told her that Maggie and Mishka mean everything to me. My happiness doesn't come from material possessions – it comes on four paws, and gives excellent kisses!

If we can all be more Maggie, we will change the world – one kind word, one smile, and one hug at a time.

ACKNOWLEDGEMENTS

Thank you to Roxanna, Maggie's guardian angel.

Thank you to Nikki Tibbles and the whole of the Wild at Heart Foundation team.

Thank you to Jordan Paramor, Ben Clark at The Soho Agency, and to Ajda Vucicevic, George Robarts and all the Mirror Books team.

And thank you to everyone in Lebanon who were a part of Maggie's rescue journey – especially Hussein!